THREADS

One family's unlikely adventure in business, mission and church planting

----

ARLENE RICHARDSON

Threads: One Family's Unlikely Adventure in Business, Mission and Church Planting

By Arlene Richardson

© 2012 by Arlene Richardson

Scriptures marked NIV taken from the HOLY BIBLE, NEW INTERNA-TIONAL VERSION®. NIV®. Copyright © 1973, 1978, 1984 by International Bible Society. All rights reserved.

Scriptures marked NLT taken from the Holy Bible, New Living Translation copyright © 1996 by Tyndale Charitable Trust. Used by permission of Tyndale House Publishers.

Trade paperback ISBN: 978-0-9852192-1-5
Ebook ISBN: 978-0-9852192-2-2

Cover design by Eric Powell
Cover photo by Chinthaka Abeyratne

The names of most people and places in this book have been changed to protect the identity of those who carry on the work.

BottomLine Media, an imprint of Pioneers, publishes materials that celebrate the "bottom line" of God's covenant with Abraham: "I will bless all nations through you." To purchase other BottomLine titles, visit *Pioneers.org/Store.*

Pioneers is an international movement that mobilizes teams to initiate church-planting movements among unreached people groups. To get involved, visit *Pioneers.org.*

PRAISE FOR THREADS

Arlene Richardson does us a favor by reminding us in her book, *Threads*, that it is possible to bring people from diverse viewpoints and religious perspectives together for a common good. Writing from the perspective that God might use her efforts to make a difference in the lives of unreached peoples, Arlene takes a step of faith and launches HeartCraft ... and the impact is powerful. Read this book expecting God to use you, too, even when you least expect it.

— Bob Creson, President/CEO
Wycliffe Bible Translators USA

Threads tells the inspiring tale of one woman's adventure that became the genesis for business as missions. Arlene Richardson's story is one of faith, innovation and love that continues to impact lives around the world.

— Ken Burenga, Former President & Chief Operating Officer
Dow Jones & Company

In a world of unreached people groups and growing hostility to a Christian witness, marketplace ministries are becoming more and more relevant in making the gospel accessible to the nations. *Threads* is the intriguing account of a young missionary who launched a grassroots business enterprise long before it was recognized as a valid methodology. The reader will be inspired to read how God worked through cross-cultural adjustments and personal challenges to reach the hearts of the people. Not only did the gospel take root through this innovative vision, it continues to flourish, as does the business.

— Jerry Rankin, President Emeritus
International Mission Board, Southern Baptist Cconvention

In her new book, *Threads*, Arlene Richardson beautifully captures the creativity and challenge involved in the cross-cultural missionary enterprise. In her down-to-earth, conversational style, Arlene relates the thrilling story of a quilt-making venture that has grown into a business enterprise which has provided employment and spiritual hope to thousands of people in the developing world. Set against the backdrop of a larger effort to reach the as yet unreached, it is a poignant story filled with adventure and color. *Threads* comes from Arlene's heart and is squarely aimed at our hearts. Reading it enlarged my vision for the unreached and heightened my passion for the work of Christ in the world.

— Dr. Jim Stevens, Senior Pastor
Christ Community Church, West Chester, Pennsylvania

What a blessing! *Threads* is the thrilling story of what God can do when ordinary people follow him in obedience and trust to venture not only into new contexts and relationships, but into new and innovative undertakings for which they feel totally inadequate except for God's faithful and directing presence with them ... and of the incredible ripple impact that such a venture can have in bringing together people continents apart to advance God's purposes among the least-reached peoples of the world.

— Gary R. Corwin
Missiologist, serving with the International Office of SIM
Associate Editor, Evangelical Missions Quarterly

More than a great God-story of a unique international business adventure among Muslims that required vision, entrepreneurship, persistence, partnership and prayer, this page-turner also breaks new ground. Of the current top 25 books on Business as Mission (BAM), all are authored by males! What a welcome addition, and contribution Arlene Richardson makes to this growing body of literature with her engaging book, *Threads*.

— Tom Steffen
Cook School of Intercultural Studies, Biola University.
Co-author with Steve Rundle of Great Commission Companies

Threads is a modern-day version of the loaves and fishes miracle. Arlene Richardson tells her amazing journey of watching God turn some old, forgotten scraps of fabric into an industry that blesses the nations. May our Lord weave a tapestry composed of thousands of similar businesses focused on the world's unreached that produce eternal results for the Kingdom of God.

— Debby Jones, speaker & author
Lady in Waiting: Becoming God's Best While Waiting for Mr. Right

Threads is a powerful autobiographical account of the life and work of the "Quilt Lady," Arlene Richardson, and her family's decade of life, work, business and ministry in Southeast Asia. Readers be warned: this is a real page-turner. Block some time for this one. You won't want to leave it until you are finished. Much more than a superb BAM (Business as Mission) case study, this is the story of a faith journey to share the transforming truth of Jesus Christ with a persecuted people who had never embraced the gospel. It is packed with life's lessons and God's blessings— prayer, faith, grace, obedience, miracles, sacrifice, suffering, and more. Thanks, Arlene, for this one. My students will love it!

— *Mike Barnett, Ph.D., Dean, College of Intercultural Studies*
Columbia International University

This is a must read for anyone thinking about doing cross cultural ministry among unreached people groups. Arlene Richardson tells her spellbinding story of how God surprised her, by using the business she founded to bless others and start a movement of people becoming followers of Jesus. You will laugh, cry and shout for joy as you relive this exciting story of obedience and victory!"

— *Durwood Snead, Director of globalX*
North Point Community Church, Alpharetta, Georgia

Easy to read, intriguing and a fresh look at the reality of one woman's steps of faith to make an eternal difference. This is a must read for any woman who seeks to be a Proverbs 31 woman and make her life count for Christ.

— *Bob Sjogren*
President, UnveilinGlory

Threads will keep you reading like a gripping novel. This is the true-life experience of a young missionary wife seeking to follow God's desire to meet the physical and spiritual needs of an unreached Muslim people group. The resulting successful ministry presents a strong case study usable as a text in intercultural studies. *Threads* incidentally demonstrates the outworking of the core values of Pioneers.

— *Dr. Edwin L. (Jack) Frizen, Jr.*
Mission Consultant, Pioneers

CONTENTS

PART 1

PART 2

PART 3

TO AN AMAZING FATHER

Dad, you urged me to write this story years ago. Thank you for "giving me the world" (Psalm 2:8) and encouraging me each step along the way. I'm sure you're still cheering me on from heaven.

FOREWORD

What a story! Or, I should say, hundreds of stories! You'll laugh. You'll cry. You'll find it difficult to put this book down. In this well-written story, you'll be intrigued as mystery after mystery unfolds.

So what is *Threads* all about? The biography of a remarkable young American who pioneered a profitable industry among a Muslim people, giving hope to those who had lost all hope? Yes, but so much more. Woven throughout *Threads* you'll find the story of tragedy and triumph in the life of another young woman, Dewi. But there's more. You'll feel the excitement of how God can impact the spiritual and material lives of people in a very different culture through a couple of young American missionaries who, in love, worked hard to bridge the gaps. And as a bonus, you'll be able to trace the multi-generational beginning of America's fastest growing mission agency.

Thank you, Arlene, for giving us a masterful recounting of God's unfolding purpose in your life.

— *J. Robertson McQuilkin*
President Emeritus
Columbia International University

INTRODUCTION

S oon after my husband Steve and I were married, we did something crazy. We packed our bags and headed overseas. No, I'm not talking about our honeymoon. We literally moved to Southeast Asia, intending to sink roots there, raise a family and make a difference in a part of the world where people have greater needs and fewer blessings.

For Steve, this wasn't such a big deal. He'd grown up with cannibals and headhunters in the jungles of New Guinea. His father's classic bestseller, *Peace Child,* tells his family's remarkable story. For me, however, this would mean a completely new life. I had grown up enjoying the best of America. My father was a successful Wall Street executive. Would I be able to adjust, much less thrive, in a foreign culture?

Boarding our flight in Los Angeles, I felt a curious mix of emotions. Steve and I were in our early twenties. Our decision to leave behind the comforts and privileges of America would trigger an irreversible domino effect. I'd need to master new languages, learn how to cook local food, give birth to my children in relatively primitive conditions and raise a family without the usual conveniences.

My fears were real, yet I felt a profound sense of peace. I was never one to settle for the tried and true. I'd always wanted my life to count. Fastening my seatbelt, I knew the time had come. Our faith would have to sustain us through the twists and turns, the highs and the lows, of the ride ahead.

Days later we found ourselves in a radically different world. To protect various individuals and the ongoing work, in this book I call these wonderful people the Kantoli and their country Nusandia.

Threads traces our adventure in the days and years that followed. It is the story of two young women from sharply contrasting backgrounds whose lives merge in friendship; how a box of quilt scraps from Punxsutawney, Pennsylvania, transformed an Asian community; how small people and small things are made great in the hands of God. It is my experience of faith, hope and love in a world of competing priorities and clashing civilizations.

PART ONE

Chapter 1

SPECIAL DELIVERY

- - - - - - - -

*It was by faith that Abraham obeyed when God called him to
leave home and go to another land that God would give him as his
inheritance. He went without knowing where he was going.
And even when he reached the land God promised him, he lived
there by faith—for he was like a foreigner, living in a tent.*

—HEBREWS 11:8-9 NLT

I t's here, Arlene!" My teammate Brenda came through our
front door carrying a huge package that she had carried all
the way from the U.S. to our home in Nusandia. Brenda quickly
said her goodbyes and left me and my dear Nusandian friend
Dewi to open the box together. We sat on the floor and carefully
removed layers of tape and paper, then cut through the cardboard to open the box. Inside were two patchwork quilts.

I caught my breath when I saw them for the first time. To
some people it might seem ridiculous to send heavy quilts to the

tropics, where we lived, but to me they were beautiful—not just because of the careful workmanship that was evident in every stitch, but also because of what they represented. They were a part of my history, my heritage. What a joy to hold these quilts for the first time after many months of anticipation!

I had almost forgotten all about those scraps from Grandma's antique furniture shop, hidden away in my parents' attic. While in the U.S. a few months earlier, I had rediscovered them. They were so beautiful—as if begging to be made into a treasure of lasting value. Was there someone who could help me make something wonderful of them? Someone who had the time and skill to sew them into a quilt for me?

I was ready to abandon the idea or leave it for some future date when I was older and had more time on my hands—when suddenly a thought occurred to me. A few weeks later, Steve and I were scheduled to visit a group of people in North Carolina. These friends prayed regularly for our work in Nusandia. They called themselves the Senders. Perhaps these dear ladies might also be interested in sewing some quilts. I had heard that North Carolinians were experts at quilting, having pioneered some of the early American designs that are still famous today. Just in case, I decided to take the scraps along. If it worked out, this would be a wonderful way for me to remember Grandma Fletcher.

When we arrived in North Carolina I found out that many of the ladies we were meeting with were quilters. In fact, they had their own quilting group! The Senders gladly received my box of fabric scraps and were excited to help with this project. We agreed that when they finished the quilts, they would send them to my mother in Virginia, who would then find a way to send them to me in Nusandia. I couldn't wait to hold a quilt in my hands made from scraps of fabric found in Grandma's antique shop.

Months later on the other side of the world, I was holding not just one quilt that these precious women had made, but two of them. Dewi, too, was amazed. She was my dearest Nusandian friend—the one I had prayed for since I moved to this wonderful remote country to live and work among her Kantoli people. It was so appropriate that she was there with me to enjoy this moment.

Dewi sat there silent for a while on the floor with me, holding the quilts and examining them. As we admired the handiwork, I told Dewi about early American pioneer women who would take old scraps of cloth, or even old feed sacks, and make something beautiful out of them in order to keep warm in the winter.

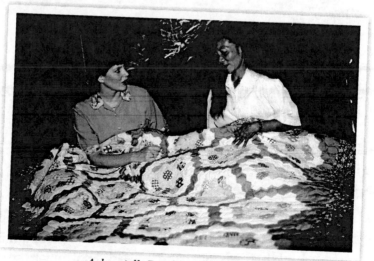

Arlene tells Dewi the story of the quilts.

Although Dewi had never experienced winter weather, she understood. I told her how quilts like these were family heirlooms that were passed down from generation to generation—pieces of art. I told her about the various creative patterns that were made and how some areas were known for certain styles,

17

patterns or colors in their quilts, such as the Amish people whose distinct patterns were known all over the United States. I explained that ladies would gather around quilting tables and talk while stitching. It was work, entertainment, art and relationship, all rolled up into one activity.

Dewi took it all in with delight and fascination. "This really fits with the Kantoli personality," she said. "We love to work with our hands, and we have the patience to do something like this."

Then she paused and looked at me. "Can you teach me how to make one of these?"

I looked at Dewi and smiled. How could I resist?

"I don't have the faintest idea," I laughed, "but we'll learn together."

✄

When Steve and I first arrived in Nusandia in 1986, Roger and Jan Casey met us at the airport outside the capital city. No one who saw us embrace in the crowded waiting area would have guessed that we were meeting each other for only the second time. To Steve and me, Roger and Jan were heroes. They had lived and worked, virtually alone, among the Kantoli people for more than 20 years.

Loading our four suitcases into the back of their Land Rover, we started the four-hour drive into the island's fertile highlands. Potholed mountain roads, dust and noise did nothing to dampen our enthusiasm and chatter. The volcanic grandeur and spectacular terraced rice fields reinforced our sense that God had led us to a new homeland—a place we would come to love and enjoy.

That evening in Denalia, the biggest city in the Kantoli part of the island, Steve and I rented a room in a youth hostel near the university. The accommodations were crowded and rudimentary, but they would serve our needs while we searched for a more permanent home.

The Caseys were affirming and helpful, but they were determined to let us find our own way. They knew from past experience that too much handholding could impede our critical introduction into the local culture. A balanced approach would make all the difference to our long-term success.

Steve and Arlene with Jan and Roger Casey

In its better years, Denalia had been a colonial resort town, surrounded by tea plantations, therapeutic hot springs and rice fields. Now it was one of the most densely populated cities in Southeast Asia—a noisy, congested home for more than two million people. Denalia's main redeeming factor was its elevation. The city was just high enough to take the edge off the equatorial heat and humidity.

A steaming volcano, which the local people affectionately called the "capsized boat," stood watch over the city. When would this volcano, one of more than a hundred volcanoes on the island, choose to erupt? I brushed the thought aside quickly, reminding myself that I had more immediate concerns.

Three days after our arrival in Nusandia, we faced our first significant challenge and responsibility—a group of nine college students from the U.S. joined us. They were volunteers who wanted to spend their summer experiencing a foreign culture. Steve and I had barely stepped off the plane ourselves. We were only a couple of years older than they were. We didn't have a home yet. We didn't know how to get around. We didn't speak the language. Steve remembered just a little of the national language from his years at a childhood boarding school in a distant part of the country. What were we thinking?

The American team joined us in the hostel, along with dozens of Nusandian students who happened to be lodging there. Not knowing what else to do, at our first official team meeting, we challenged the team to make friends with the Kantoli.

"Your goal is to go out in pairs onto the city streets, meet people, build friendships and get yourselves invited to stay in Kantoli homes for the next few weeks," Steve explained. "You have six more days to do this. You can't stay in this youth hostel more than one week."

The team was incredulous, but after we talked it over and prayed about it, they all agreed to take up the challenge. Was there any better way to trust God and learn the Kantoli culture than to live in their homes?

Five of the team members were young ladies, all very attractive. In a Muslim culture, this complicated things considerably. One of them, Gayle, had signed up for the program with very little idea where she was going. She was a belle from Atlanta with a captivating smile. Stepping off the plane, Gayle's face betrayed her dismay as she took in the sights, sounds and smells around her. I wondered how she would cope during the next six weeks.

It wasn't long before I had my answer. A couple of days later, the students stopped in a city square to have their picture taken with some Nusandian university friends. Just as the camera clicked, a young man standing next to Gayle leaned over and kissed her on the cheek. The Nusandians who were standing around cheered and clapped—especially the guys. They had seen such beauty only in the movies. Here was a real, live Western woman. One of them had successfully kissed her and had a picture to prove it.

Gayle made no effort to hide her disgust. "What kind of a place is this?" she protested. I tried to reassure her and encourage her to hang in there until she figured out how to navigate her new surroundings. My words seemed to fall on deaf ears, and I couldn't blame her. I was feeling disgusted myself.

That night, Gayle and the four other American girls piled into their room at the youth hostel. The room had several bunk beds in it. Before going to bed, I spent some time with the girls to reflect on the day and see how they were doing in their cultural adjustment—but I had another agenda as well.

On our way to Nusandia a week earlier, the plane Steve and I were on had stopped in Honolulu to refuel. Wandering through the shops in the terminal, I noticed a small candy shop. To my delight, on one of the shelves, I saw a big piece of black licorice shaped perfectly like a life-sized rat! I was thrilled. This was the ideal snack to take with me to Nusandia. I had been told that Nusandia had lots of rats. One way or another, an extra rat might prove useful.

As the girls and I relaxed and recounted the day's adventures (and misadventures), I reached into my pocket and pulled out the big black licorice rat that I'd brought from Hawaii. Discreetly, I slipped it under the sheets of Gayle's bed. No one noticed a thing.

A few minutes later, I excused myself and rejoined Steve in our own nearby room. I told him what I'd done. Steve just shook his head and smiled as we waited for the inevitable. I told him to stay quiet no matter what.

A team of students from the U.S.

A half hour later, we heard a shriek. I buried my head in my pillow trying to contain my laughter. The screams got louder and louder. Finally we leaped out of bed and rushed to the scene. Young men and women were running from other parts of the dormitory. Soon they were joined by a large group of young men who had been watching a late-night European soccer game in the lobby. In no time at all, there was a large crowd outside the door of the girls' room. Gayle was in the corner with her hand over her mouth, and the other girls were jumping up and down on their beds, trying to get as far as they could from Gayle's bed.

The crowd of Americans and Nusandians pressed closer. Ashley, one of the bravest of the girls, flung back Gayle's bed sheet. There, near the foot of the bed, was a big, ugly rat! Apparently injured or dazed, it lay there motionless.

One of the young men on the team pushed his way to the front of the crowd and strode into the girl's room. It was Joe, playfully nicknamed "Ramjo" by the Nusandians because he reminded them of Sylvester "Rambo" Stallone—compact and muscular. The room had a big window into the hallway. Spectators crowded around the window to get a glimpse of the action. Sensing an opportunity to showcase his manhood, Ramjo walked over to the bed and leaned over to get a closer look. He hesitated for just a moment, and then swiftly jerked the injured rat into the air by its tail. As another chorus of screams reverberated through the halls, Ramjo lowered its flailing body headfirst into his mouth.

By this time, even the Nusandians were horrified. Ramjo bit off the head of the rat and chewed on it. Then he feverishly chewed on its body, until only the long tail dangled from his mouth. The Nusandian students, no strangers to rats themselves, were amazed that an American would kill a rat with his bare hands and then proceed to eat its uncooked head and body!

My practical joke had succeeded beyond my wildest dreams. Even the Nusandians had fallen for it. As things began to quiet down, Steve and I slipped back into our room. Steve again just shook his head, wondering what kind of damage control he'd need to do the next day.

After we went to bed, the girls realized I was the one to blame for their humiliation. Joe confessed the rat was nothing more than a delicious candy snack. The Nusandians, however, were harder to convince. "Licorice rat" wasn't part of their vocabulary. They are probably still telling their children the story today.

During our first few weeks in Nusandia, I had many more opportunities to play pranks on these courageous young students. Though they tried often, they never succeeded in taking revenge on me. We found the laughter and fun to be a marvelous antidote for the stress and culture shock that swept over all of us from time to time.

Our student team had an amazing experience that summer. All of them were adopted by Nusandian families and built deep relationships. They learned much of the language and had opportunities to share their lives and their faith with their host families. When it came time for the students to return to America, a large crowd of people saw them off at the train station, many of them with tears streaming down their faces. I was amazed and silently thanked God for accomplishing more in their lives than Steve and I had ever dreamed possible.

When our train arrived in the capital city of Nusandia that night, we looked for an inexpensive place to stay. The students were scheduled to catch a flight home early the next morning. The small "hotel" we picked out had big rats going up and down the stairs, and lots of cockroaches and mosquitoes. The young Americans, despite their many learning experiences during the preceding weeks, were feeling watchful and edgy.

After dinner, the girls announced that they were going out on a last-minute shopping excursion to pick up some souvenirs. They invited me along, but I told them I needed a break. I hadn't misbehaved for a long time, and I sensed that the time was right to strike again.

Days earlier, I had bought a big rubber gorilla mask from a roadside vendor. After the girls left, I grabbed my gorilla mask and slipped into their room. This time I crept into their closet and closed the door behind me. Donning the mask and putting a dark towel over my head and shoulders, I squatted on the floor of the closet behind the clothes and baggage.

After sweating in the cramped darkness of the closet for about an hour, I finally heard the sound of the girls returning. As soon as they entered their room they started packing their suitcases for the long journey home. I knew it was only a matter of time now. Adrenaline surged through my arteries as I braced for action.

Suddenly one of the young ladies flung open the closet door to retrieve her clothes. Sure enough, it was Gayle. She reached in to pull a shirt off the hanger. As she shifted the hangers, I grabbed her arm and jumped out from the corner of the closet. All of the girls let out blood-curdling screams. As they fled for the door, I bounced around the room like a real live African gorilla, making noises and chasing them. It was several priceless moments before the girls regained their composure and realized they had been duped once again!

Oh the joys of those who love humor. It truly is the spice of life. Somehow I knew we'd need large doses of it in the months and years ahead as we settled into our new lives among the Kantoli. This was no place for the faint of heart. The challenges and spiritual battles we were already beginning to experience were only too real. Other people had come, tried and failed. Would we be any different?

Chapter 2

NEW BEGINNINGS

- - - - - - - -

*Do not despise these small beginnings, for the Lord rejoices to
see the work begin.*

—Zechariah 4:10 NLT

Ill-prepared as we were to receive them, the student team
turned out to be a huge blessing. Through their host families,
we became acquainted with many Kantoli people. Three of the
nine college students would later return to live and work with
us. One of them, Jada, met Steve's cousin after she returned to
the U.S. They got married and joined us in Nusandia a few years
later. As for Gayle, to her great credit, she persevered and ended
up having a very positive experience.

With the team on its way home, Steve and I turned our attention more fully to our own needs and plans. One priority was
finding a permanent home. We weren't as concerned with the
house itself as we were with its location. We wanted to be in a
thoroughly Kantoli neighborhood.

Nusandia has many people groups and cultures. As many as 800 languages are spoken across the country. Each language represents a specific people group and culture. Most Nusandians speak at least two languages—their mother tongue and the national Nusandian language. The Kantoli are one of the largest people groups in Nusandia and have their own homeland in this part of the island. Though Denalia is located in their area, people from many other ethnic groups moved to the city over the years. We knew we would have to make a special effort to live among the Kantoli if we really wanted to identify with them.

Before long, the Caseys suggested a house in a densely populated part of Denalia. I fell in love with it. It was ideal for us because it was in an area that was culturally Kantoli. We signed a one-year lease for $1,000 and moved in immediately.

We loved walking through the narrow alleyways to reach the home. About 3,000 people lived within three or four blocks. Nearby was a bustling market. The community was so crowded that our house even shared the same wall with our neighbor. From our window we could look into our neighbor's living room, and from the second floor, we could look down onto a sea of clay tile rooftops.

As the days morphed into weeks, Steve and I began to feel more and more comfortable. Every new day brought unexpected tests and experiences. It was stressful, but we were learning fast. We enjoyed the challenge of immersing ourselves in a new language and culture.

In front of our home was a very narrow street, barely wide enough for a car to squeeze through. The Dedeng family lived directly across the street from us. Mr. Dedeng was the patriarch and government-designated leader in the community. His job was to watch the neighborhood carefully, ensure harmony and security and keep everyone in line politically. We found Mr. and

Mrs. Dedeng to be very nice people. They sensed our vulnerability and quickly took us into their protective care.

The Dedengs were middle class. They had two homes—this one in the city and another on a rice farm that they owned about a four hours' drive into the mountains. They had eight daughters. In the Kantoli culture (as in most Muslim cultures), boys are much preferred over girls. The Dedengs had tried for a boy, over and over, and had never succeeded. Finally, they counted their losses and gave up. We enjoyed meeting all their beautiful girls.

The view from our back porch.

Just outside our house on the right was a dusty, open lot where children played and flew their kites. Kite "fighting" was a favorite pastime. This field was the community gathering place where people would have special functions and celebra-

29

tions such as Independence Day, Idul Fitri (the Muslim holiday marking the end of Ramadan), or Idul Adha (the Muslim holiday commemorating when Abraham nearly sacrificed his son). On certain Islamic holy days, goats and cows would be slaughtered right next to our house. We were at the center of it all, and we loved it. We could see and hear everything.

Our little community had five mosques. After we arrived, their loudspeakers were mysteriously redirected toward our home. They would blast us out of bed at four o'clock each morning. The noon, afternoon and evening calls to prayer were sad and eerie to my uninitiated ears.

It wasn't long after we moved in that one of the "mothers" of the community invited me to join their choral group. They were preparing for a big performance on Nusandian Independence Day. I don't consider myself a very good singer in English, much less in someone else's language, yet I was honored by the invitation. When I arrived for practice, about 25 ladies had already gathered. They went around the circle introducing themselves to me. When they finished, one of the oldest women, who seemed to be in charge, asked me to go around the circle and recall their names by memory. I quickly realized they wanted to have some fun at my expense.

Next the ladies asked me to sing a solo in their language. They were making a monkey out of me! I wasn't enjoying myself nearly as much as they were. It was obvious I didn't know what I was doing, and they found tremendous humor in my bumbling attempts to sing in their language. I felt silly and just wanted to go home, but I decided to stay. I had to learn how to be a good sport. After the jokes I had played on the American college girls, I probably deserved this treatment.

When Independence Day finally came, our choral group performed in front of 1,000 people crowded into the empty lot next to our home. I managed to sing along, much to the throng's delight. The tall white American stuck out like a sore thumb, but I had a lot of fun, and it gave me a wonderful opportunity to meet my neighbors.

Steve was enrolled as a student at one of the state universities. He even had a scholarship to cover tuition costs, though we had to cover our own living expenses. Since we were still in our twenties, we blended into the university setting quite well. Steve studied the national Nusandian language the first year, the local Kantoli language the second year and Islamic history the third year. He also had an opportunity to do some field research on the Kantoli language with a team of students.

Steve enjoyed speaking to his new friends in their own language.

Like me, Steve began spending time with people who lived around us, although he had to fit this between classes at the university. One day he ventured down the alley behind our home where many poor people lived. Their homes teetered on a cliff overlooking a river that was brown with silt and garbage. Sometimes the men would set up a dilapidated ping-pong table in the alley for recreation. Steve loved table tennis, and he figured he could practice his language while playing table tennis with the men.

That evening we had a knock at the door. It was Asep, a neighbor who prided himself on being an English teacher at the nearby elementary school. We tried not to let on that we couldn't understand his English. Switching to Nusandian, Asep chided Steve for playing table tennis with the people who lived behind us. He said it was inappropriate for Steve, an educated person of high standing, to play table tennis with the lower-class people living in the back section of the community. Steve should stick with upper-class friends and not mingle with people of lower status.

I felt a bit offended by Asep's comments about the neighbors behind us. It was ironic to me that Asep, a poor man himself by Western standards, would look down his nose at people who lived on the street behind him. It made me realize how stratified Kantoli society is. There was a lot of Hindu influence from India in Nusandia's past. Though not as pronounced as in India, there appeared to be a caste system of some kind here, too.

As a Christian, my heart told me that all people are created equal and we're not to regard one person more highly than another. Jesus spent time with people of all economic groups, backgrounds and cultures. If Jesus visited our community, would He play ping-pong with the men in the back alley? Of course He would. In fact, I felt we were to go out of our way to befriend the poor. Jesus defied many of the conventions of His own culture. He could have lived in a palace, but instead chose the life of a peasant.

Even the Kantoli language itself, I quickly found, reinforced inequalities between people. There are five different levels of vocabulary to choose from whenever you want to say anything, depending on the status of the person you are talking to. The lowest level of language is the one that you would use when referring to really poor people or to animals. While I wanted to respect the culture, I also wanted to truly communicate the love of Christ. There would be times when I would need to defy some of these conventions, I decided. Every culture has its blind spots.

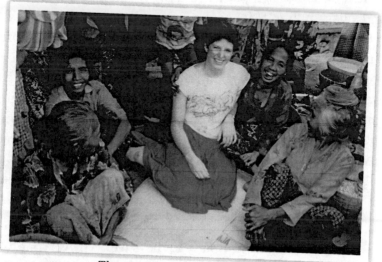

The women treated me like a celebrity.

The majority of Kantoli people live in mountain villages. They are wet rice farmers. Steve and I had come to "seek and to save that which was lost" (Luke 19:10). We would be respectful, but we wouldn't let social expectations prevent us from reaching out to those with the greatest need.

I enrolled in a formal language program and practiced my language every opportunity I had, on the public transport and walking the streets and visiting my neighbors. Steve had an advantage because he had spent his childhood in another part of the country. He had grown up speaking a tribal language, and his ear was already familiar with Nusandian, so he was picking it up faster than I was. He was determined not to let me rely too much on his ability in the language. One day we agreed that I would go across town by myself for my language lesson. I wanted to prove to Steve that I could do it. I wrote our new address on a piece of paper and put it in my pocket. Steve wished me well and off I went.

It took almost an hour of riding in the back of several hot and dusty public transport vehicles before I finally reached the school where I had my lesson. After about three hours of study, I went back out onto the street and started my journey home. Unfortunately, I got on the wrong public transport. After awhile, nothing looked familiar. I rode around the city for a long time while dozens of people were getting on and off the noisy, open-air transport. I even went through the main bus station downtown where hundreds of people were milling around. I started to get concerned as nothing looked like my street. It brought back memories of when I'd gotten lost on the wrong school bus as a little girl.

I relayed my address verbally to the driver, but everyone on the bus had a different opinion of where that street was! They looked at me like I was from another planet. Was my accent not adequate for him to understand? I showed the driver and other passengers my address on the paper. They all rattled off more of the language that I did not know. Never before had I felt more like Dorothy in the *Wizard of Oz* when she clicked her red shoes and kept saying, "There's no place like home." I just wanted to go home!

Darkness was closing in fast. After clattering around the city for a long time, I started to see rice paddies on the right and left. I knew that I was in trouble—I was heading out of the city! I had been praying but decided to pray even harder. Was Steve worried about me?

I motioned to the driver, insisting that he turn around and head back to the center of town. He took me back to the station and we started over again. Just then, another person got on the vehicle and looked at the address on my paper. He knew exactly where that little road was. I never felt more relief than at that moment. Before too long I saw the familiar scene of the market at the end of our road. I thanked the driver for getting me home and gave him a generous tip for his efforts.

Our garage, filled with food, in preparation for a wedding

I was safely home, and I had conquered the impossible—using public transport all over the city with very little language. What about Steve? He was a little bit worried about me but commented that it was another good learning experience to add to my list!

One day the leading women of our community asked if they could use our home to cook for a wedding. Ati, the second of the Dedengs' eight daughters, was to be married that weekend. It sounded like a great opportunity, so I said yes. A few hours later the women arrived with their pots and pans. Cartloads of supplies were unloaded at our front door. Women were all over our house. They cooked all day and all night. Then they cooked all the next day. Food that had been cooked the day before just sat on the sidelines, collecting flies. I wondered to myself if this might be the reason that our stomachs so often churned when we ate food at community events. I watched it all with fascination. It was an incredible experience being with these women who were chattering away and having the time of their lives preparing for this special event.

Usually I loved being in a tight-knit community, but sometimes it was a real challenge. Every culture has a different boundary for personal space, and I was realizing that my boundaries were quite different than the Kantoli's. Often, for example, our neighbors would walk into our home unannounced. One time we were leaving town for a few days, and we asked Mr. Dedeng, across the alley from us, to keep an eye on our home. A few minutes after we left, I realized I had forgotten something, so we turned around and headed back to our house. When we went in, we found Mr. Dedeng in our kitchen, examining the canned goods in the cupboards. He was curious to know what kind of food we were buying and how much we were spending on it. He looked a bit embarrassed that we had caught him snooping around in our house. He told Steve he was just checking to see if we had locked all the windows.

Cultural differences were apparent in other ways, too. One time our next-door neighbor, Mr. Ardi, came to our front door hauling a shiny, bulky television. It was so big that he had to have another man help bring it into our house. Without any explanation, he began to set it up in our main room. We weren't sure what was going on. We hadn't asked for a television, and we didn't really even want one, even though all of our neighbors had TVs. After all, there were only three government-controlled channels available.

As Mr. Ardi plugged in the TV, Steve began asking questions.

"What are you doing, Mr. Ardi?"

"I'm installing a TV."

"Whose TV is it?"

Mr. Ardi explains his "gift" of a television.

"Why, it's yours, of course."

"Are you giving it to us?"

"Of course!"

"Wow, that's awfully nice of you."

"Don't mention it."

Ardi's generosity amazed us. Steve double-checked to make sure there were no strings attached. As Ardi left, we thanked him profusely.

A few days later Mr. Ardi knocked on our door. Clearing his throat, he asked if we could begin making payments on the TV.

"Pay for the TV?" Steve queried. "I thought you said you were giving it to us. If I was going to buy a TV, I would have chosen a smaller, cheaper one."

"Ah, yes, but surely you can afford this one. It's very nice."

"Where did you get it?"

"A man owed me money and couldn't pay me, so I went into his house and got his TV."

We'd been had. Our neighbor was using us to recoup his money from a delinquent client. We quickly realized that, even in Nusandia, nothing comes free.

On another occasion, one of our neighbors brought us a nice plate of cookies. This was one of the ladies who had mocked me when I had joined the community choir. Maybe this was her way of apologizing? What a lovely gesture! Their desire for a relationship touched our hearts.

A few days later, these same neighbors paid us another visit. Smiling with anticipation, they asked if we could arrange for their son to study at an American university. The cookies, we realized, came at a price.

The Kantoli people seemed to have frequent religious celebrations. These took some getting used to. One night we heard the boys of the community chanting all night long over the mosque loudspeaker. When this happened, we knew that another celebration was coming. Sure enough, this time it was Idul Adha, a holiday commemorating the time the prophet Abraham almost sacrificed his son Ishmael. The Bible says it was Isaac, but the Quran claims it was Ishmael.

We were exhausted from losing a full night's sleep, but eager to learn more. Early the next morning, we watched as the dirt field next to our house filled with hundreds of white-robed worshippers. The imam started praying, and everyone bowed repeatedly toward Mecca. After prayers, dozens of goats, sheep and cows were brought out and slaughtered. Steve and I watched with interest, and I thought of the scripture that says the "blood of bulls and goats" is not what the Lord requires (Hebrews 10:4). God Himself has already provided the perfect sacrifice through His Son.

Neighbors prepare goats and sheep for sacrifice.

I have to confess it was a bit sickening to watch the throats of these animals being slit. It made the reality of the Old Testament sacrificial system come alive for me. These animals stood there innocently, not knowing that in the next moment they would be yanked forward by several men and forced to lie down with their necks over an open hole full of blood. The animals would be skinned and hung up to be butchered and the meat divided among the neighbors. After a few hours, I went home hoping to take a nap. My head was pounding with a horrible headache.

Just as I was beginning to relax, there was a knock at the door. When Steve and I opened the door we found the Muslim *imam* standing there with a big platter. On the platter was the head of a goat. I was quite shocked but pretended I was used to this kind of greeting! Soon I realized that the community wanted to honor us. They had given us the best they had to offer. Of course there is only one head to every animal, so that makes a goat head extra special.

What in the world was I going to do with a goat's head? How was I supposed to fix it? Perhaps I could grill the tongue, but what about the eyes and the ears? I didn't really know how to get out of this situation without offending someone. Suddenly, I had an idea.

"We are very new here, and I don't feel we are worthy of such an honor," I explained. "Please accept our heartfelt thanks, and pass this goat's head on to one of the elders in the community."

The imam seemed to understand and appreciate what I was saying. He left with a smile, only to return a few minutes later. This time he had a huge cow's liver on the platter! He and several other men from the community came into our home and went to work chopping up the liver. They skewered the pieces with sate sticks and grilled them. It was quite an evening as the Muslim priest and other patriarchs of the community feasted on cow's liver around our small dining room table.

Although we were not particularly germ conscious, we did face plenty of bizarre medical challenges. I never had dental problems until I moved to Nusandia, but suddenly I started having lots of them. A few weeks after we arrived in the country, we borrowed a little Italian motor scooter from the Caseys.

They were taking a trip to America and wouldn't need it for a few months. The scooter was so small that when Steve and I both sat on it, the scooter itself was scarcely visible.

Kantoli greet with hands together. Arlene greets Mrs. Dedeng.

As we floated down the streets each day on our scooter, the wind and dust whipped around me, creating a lot of pain in a tooth that had developed some sensitivity. We asked our neighbors where to find a "tooth expert," and went from one to another but couldn't get satisfying answers. One night I couldn't take it any longer. The pain was excruciating. We tried yet another dentist, and she felt compassion enough to open up her office at 10 p.m. I have never been more relieved in all my life. She knew what to do and performed a root canal very quickly. Conditions were a bit primitive, but the cost was just right—only $13.00!

After all the pain eventually subsided, I felt like a new person.

A day or two later, however, I started to have second thoughts. I developed a horrific throat infection that overcame me quickly. I could not swallow, not even a bit. It all happened so quickly that I ended up in the hospital. The conclusion was that, although my root canal was cheap and quick, it probably had not been done with sterile instruments!

Later I had another episode in which a molar in my mouth deteriorated rapidly. The tooth expert (a different one) said it was "rotten" and was convinced I needed it removed. I wanted so much to keep this tooth, but I felt helpless at the hands of the dentist. Wasn't there some other way? Apparently not.

The office was packed full with people. When it was finally my turn, I was injected with a little Novocaine and instructed to wait until the painkiller had taken effect.

I waited and waited while other patients filed past me. When I finally got into the seat and the dentist started to use pliers to twist my molar out, I felt excruciating pain. I had waited so long that the anesthetic had worn off. That's why I was feeling every twist and turn of the pliers.

I quickly told the dentist that I was in terrible pain. He rushed into the next room to get another injection of Novocaine. Moments later, he returned to say that the Novocaine was *sibah*—all gone. *Sibah* is one of the first words I learned in Nusandia. It is used all the time.

All the patients before me had used up the anesthesia, and there was none left for me. My molar was already loose and bleeding. The dentist asked me what he should do. It did not make sense to leave the job half done, so I told him to go ahead without painkiller. I didn't have much choice! The dentist and his assistant had to hold me down and extract my molar. I went home crying and hoping that I would never have another dental problem ever again.

Chapter 3

TRIALS & TREASURES

- - - - - - - -

Feed the hungry and help those in trouble.
Then your light will shine out from the darkness, and the
darkness around you will be as bright as day.

—ISAIAH 58:10-11 NLT

Steve and I both wore wedding rings, but our neighbors did not seem convinced that we were really married. First, wedding rings didn't mean anything to them. Second, they'd heard that American "infidels" live together and don't bother getting married. Most tellingly, in Kantoli culture, if you are married, the first thing you do is have children—and Steve and I had no children. We'd been waiting for life to settle down. The idea of waiting to have children was foreign to our neighbors. They kept asking us if we were using birth control, and, if so, what kind? I wasn't used to these kinds of questions, especially in a large group setting. I realized these are topics of everyday conversation for the Kantoli. In their country, there had been a big push to control the population.

Huge billboards announced, "Two kids are enough!" Part of this push involved educating the population about birth control. Over the years, this had become a topic of everyday conversation.

Much to our friends' relief, a few months after we moved into their community, I became pregnant. Suddenly our neighbors were all smiles, and everyone anxiously awaited the new arrival. My Nusandian doctor assured me that was a safe place to have a baby. "Thousands of them are born here every year," he said with a grin. "It's nothing new."

When time came for delivery, Steve drove me to a small clinic in a nicer part of town. The delivery room was simple. The table was hard and covered with a plastic sheet. The doctor took his gloves out of a used cookie tin on the shelf. There was no air conditioning, and insects swarmed freely. No one seemed to worry about it except my mother, who had flown over from America for the occasion.

My labor was long and difficult. After about 24 hours, I was completely drained. The midwives kept commenting on how long it was taking me compared to Nusandian women. Two Nusandian babies were born in the room next to me while I was on the delivery table. Finally the doctor decided to use some kind of European vacuum machine to pull my baby out by the head. Since I had never had a baby before, I had nothing to compare my experience with.

Our beautiful daughter Joy was born in October 1987. I cradled her in my arms with tears of exhaustion and relief streaming down my face. I had been through so much. Joy's head seemed a bit bruised from the suction process, but otherwise she seemed to be fine. My mother and Steve looked much relieved. Joy was a gorgeous little baby.

I spent five days recuperating in the Nusandian birthing clinic. The total cost for everything came to about $400. I was given VIP treatment with a bucket of hot water at five a.m. and an assortment of local delicacies for meals. I was even served the local favorite: curried chicken intestines.

Our neighbors were delighted that I had chosen to have my baby born on Kantoli soil. They love children more than anything else, and the Kantoli called Joy their *mojang priyangan* or "little Kantoli girl." The Dedengs were pleased that we'd had a girl. After all, they had eight of them. It was fine that we'd had a girl this time, they told us, since we'd have other opportunities in the future to have a boy.

Neighbors soon flooded our home. What do Americans feed their babies? What was she wearing? How was I holding her? Why did the baby sleep in her own little bed? How lonely that must be! On and on it went. I would put Joy to sleep only to have her awakened by curious neighbors who wanted to hold her and rock her. Sometimes mothers would stick their fingers in Joy's mouth to see if she had any teeth yet. Often when I returned home, I would see a pile of shoes at the front door, indicating that there were visitors waiting to see baby Joy.

Not long after she was born, Joy started getting a lot of stomach pain right after her last feeding of the day. Sometimes she would cry until about two in the morning. This went on for quite some time. I was so sleep deprived that I would give the baby to Steve, and he would wait up with her and try to rock her to sleep. No one had ever told me how bad colic could be. Joy seemed to have an especially bad case of it. I thought that babies just ate and slept, but I was wrong.

Joy's cries could not be muffled in the night, and our neighbors could hear almost every move we made. Ardi's home shared a wall with ours, and the Dedengs were just a few meters away. My neighbors were convinced that as a first-time mother I needed help. Apparently their babies never got colic. Well-meaning friends and neighbors came up with all kinds of herbal concoctions that would help the baby or me. What I really needed was sleep, but what I got were countless knocks at the door from the senior women of the community. They were older and wiser and wanted to tell me about how to take care of a baby. Others brought strange leaves and herbs, which they seemed quite sure would help. Others rubbed strange smelling oil on Joy's little stomach.

Worst of all, the ladies were horrified to realize that the baby was not sleeping in the same bed with me. She must be lonely and cold, they said. Adding to their dismay, I put Joy down on her stomach when she slept. Everyone felt they had the answers for why Joy was not doing well at night. "Eat this, do that, turn her this way, hold her that way." Even Steve's professors at the university were giving him advice.

The convergence of all these experiences and the physical and emotional toll of giving birth to Joy and adjusting to a new environment brought on a strong culture shock that I had not had before and have never had since. We had been in the country almost a year and a half, and I was by this time quite fluent in the Nusandian language, although I didn't speak much Kantoli yet. We had many friendships and kept up a very busy schedule of guests and projects, yet I felt waves of weariness. I desperately wanted personal space in order to take care of my precious baby daughter. The novelty of being in another country had long since worn off for me. Now I felt like I was just barely surviving. Tears came easily, and to complicate matters, I had a serious case of post-partum depression. Emotionally, I felt I was in one of the deepest valleys I'd ever been in.

It encouraged me to know that many Kantoli people appreciated us and loved our family. Our presence among them hadn't gone unnoticed. They had truly embraced us into their lives and community. Steve was a constant presence and help to me, and we appreciated the affirmation of our growing network of American friends and family members, too.

Over time, Joy outgrew her colic, and I began to regain my bearings. Joy was strong and healthy and grew faster than most of the Kantoli babies. Our friends sometimes asked us to tell them our secret for having strong, healthy babies. Steve would smile and explain that our babies grow quickly "because they drink Coca Cola." They would look surprised and puzzled and then nod their heads as if to say, "Of course, of course. Why didn't we think of that?"

Joy liked sitting on the family's motorcycle.

A few months before Joy was born, I was walking in the community and was greeted by a woman my age. She was friendly and able to speak quite good English. To my delight she was expecting

47

her first baby, too. I invited her into my home and heard her story. Irma was a medical doctor, and we became close friends over the next few years.

Irma was honored when I would come to her for health advice or to bring a sick friend for consultation. She wondered what would motivate me to take money from my own pocket and bring these poor people to her office. She was intrigued by my personality and wondered aloud what made me different than other foreigners she had met. I was able to give her my story and explain that I was a follower of Jesus. The Lord had given me a compassion for needy people. She explained that Muslims, too, believe in giving alms to the poor. The pious ones give as much as two percent of their income to the mosque and to the poor, but what I was doing seemed very unusual and excessive.

Irma was a fun person to interact with. She was smart and inquisitive. I learned so much from her about the culture of the people. She often did not agree with my associations with the poor on the outskirts of the community, but at the same time she was impressed by my love for her people. I brought friends with tuberculosis or typhoid to her doorstep and helped them purchase the medicines they needed. To me these were small sacrifices in an environment of overwhelming need. In this fatalistic culture, I enjoyed seeing the hope of Christ break through into people's lives. People wanted to ask me spiritual questions while I was helping them. It is the love of Christ expressed in tangible ways that draws people to the message. The truth of the gospel shines brightest in those who practice random acts of kindness with no strings attached.

Irma had another favorite topic. She and her husband Tarto were fascinated by the way Steve and I related to one another. They clearly loved each other and wanted to build a solid marriage. In Islam, Irma confided, marriage is dominated by the topic of sex. They'd seen so many shallow or mechanical marriages around them and wanted their own experience to be different. More than once Irma asked me what it was like to have a Christian marriage. It gave me a great opportunity to share openly with her about the difference that the Lord Jesus can make in a person's life and marriage.

Irma and I had our first babies about the same time. We had so much in common and would often compare notes on the things we were facing in life. In fact, she was pregnant with her second child about the same time I was. During my second pregnancy, I woke up one morning to see that my ankles were horribly swollen, and I could not bend my fingers. They looked like sausages. I staggered to the mirror and stared at myself in horror. Huge, red circular welts covered my body, even on my very pregnant midsection. I looked like something out of a science fiction movie. I was swollen and in pain and itching. Every hour the welts would migrate to other parts of my body, leaving behind huge brown bruises.

Once again our neighbors flooded into the home offering various explanations and antidotes. Some said I was allergic to shrimp, and others, to caterpillars. I was growing weary from all the stares and all the advice, even though I knew they all meant well. I felt like Job in the Bible, when all his friends gathered around to speculate about the causes of his suffering. Irma was the only one who offered reasonable advice. She insisted that I see a skin specialist. When I finally found one, he examined me and said, "This is very bad."

"Yes, I know it's bad," I said. "That's why I'm here. I need help! Just how bad is it?"

"Very, very bad," he said as he shook his head. I was impatient and wanted answers. The American in me was coming out.

The doctor slid some little red pills my way. "This will help," he said. I could not get a clear answer from him as to what kind of pill they were. All I knew was that I was pregnant and should not take medication that I did not know about as it could harm the baby. I left feeling discouraged and frustrated. Then Steve had an idea: I would fly to the Baptist hospital a few hundred miles away in the eastern part of the island. We made some phone calls, but when I explained I was only a few weeks away from delivery, the doctors decided it was not smart for me to fly. I would have to gut it out and endure the pain.

The same day as my doctor's appointment, our newest co-workers, Larry and Mary Catherine, arrived in the country to join our work. Steve picked them up at the airport. When they arrived at our house and I opened the door, Mary Catherine gasped. She could hardly believe her eyes.

"Is this what's going to happen to me here in Nusandia?" she asked.

She looked like she was reconsidering her decision to move halfway around the world. I tried to reassure her, but my face was not convincing.

Until the day I delivered our second daughter, Sarah, I had welts and bruises all over my body. The doctor had never seen anything like it. Compared to Joy, Sarah's actual birth was a breeze. I had endured a horrible reaction to something for several weeks but finally delivered a healthy baby girl. A week or two after Sarah's birth, all my strange symptoms disappeared—and we never knew what brought them on in the first place.

Sarah blended right in with our family and busy lifestyle. Experts say it is probably not a good idea to have a baby during your first few years in a foreign country. The stress is great as you learn a new language and culture. I'd had two babies and found that in many ways it accelerated my adjustment. I had no choice but to survive and adapt! Our two little girls were precious, heaven-sent treasures, and we felt so blessed.

One day we got a notice in the mail saying we needed to come to the capital city to pick up a package. Some thoughtful friends back in the U.S.A. had sent us something by DHL. They assumed it would be safer and easier for us to get it special delivery, even though it would cost them a lot more to send it that way. The only problem was that DHL didn't have an office in our city of Denalia.

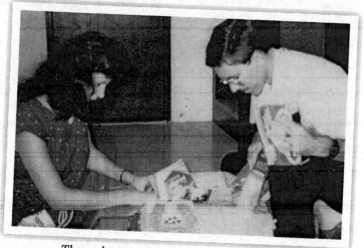

The package was great—once we finally got it!

Steve and I read the notice, looked at each other and gulped. Our friends wanted to bless us, of course, but they had no idea that, in order to pick up the package, we'd have to drive four hours each way via twisting, turning mountain roads! It would have been so much easier if they had sent it through the regular postal system. And since we didn't have a car, we'd have to hire a taxi for a full day. Not having much choice, we decided to make a day of it.

We left Denalia before daybreak the next morning and reached the capital city by mid-morning, on the tail end of the morning rush hour. Our hired car crawled the final few miles into the center of the city. When we finally found the DHL office, we were told that we'd come to the wrong place. We needed to go to the international airport, "only an hour away"!

Off we went. When we arrived at the airport, we found that it was not a simple process to pick up a package. We had to visit multiple desks, officials and smoke-filled rooms. At some offices, we asked directions. At others, we filled out forms, got stamps on our papers, showed residency documents or paid fees. After a few hours, I thought I was going nuts! To keep our sanity, we started counting the offices and windows that we visited that day. We counted 26!

When Steve and I arrived home late that night, we had spent 15 hours and about $150 picking up our package. The cake mixes, seasonings and Snickers bars that came out of it never looked so good!

✂

One of the first friends Steve made was a young man named Endamora. He and his friend Agus came to our home often and enjoyed playing board games with us. Endamora had taught himself English, and Steve soon conscripted him as a Nusandian language teacher. Each day Steve would read a Nusandian newspaper article, and they would study all the terminology together for a few hours. Although Endamora understood quite a bit of English, he would speak only Nusandian with us to help us learn his language faster. Steve would write new vocabulary words on tiny flash cards and keep them on a ring in his pocket. Whenever he was on a bus or sitting in a government office, he'd go over hundreds of vocabulary words. Using this simple approach, Steve learned fast. Within weeks, he seemed quite fluent.

One day I invited Endamora and Agus over for a Thanksgiving dinner. They were curious about American food and customs, and this would be a good opportunity to familiarize them with American culture. Remarkably, I was able to order a small turkey through an upscale store in the wealthier part of town. But as Steve was pulling the turkey out of the refrigerator, the electricity suddenly went off. Everything went pitch black. Suddenly, I heard a terrible cry from the kitchen. The turkey had slipped neck first out of Steve's hands. The wire that stuck out of the turkey's neck had plunged into Steve's big toe!

Steve pulled himself together fairly quickly, and eventually, the electrical power came back on. I began cooking the turkey. As the turkey baked in the oven, the two young men seemed to squirm uncomfortably in their seats. I assured Endamora and Agus that a turkey is just an oversized chicken and would taste very similar.

When it was finally time to eat, the two could no longer hold themselves back. No sooner did they take the first bite than they rushed out the door holding their hands over their mouths. Apparently, the taste of turkey was revolting to them. Perhaps it wasn't similar to chicken after all?

❊

Our close relationship with the Dedeng family continued to strengthen. One day they invited us to visit their ancestral home, and we travelled five hours outside the city with them. I was amazed at the remoteness of this place. It was truly Kantoli, and most of the people preferred to use only the Kantoli language rather than the national Nusandian language. What an excellent place to go deeper into the culture. The Dedengs took us to the cemetery where most of their ancestors were buried. Sitting on the stone wall that encircled the little graveyard,

I wondered how many more generations might perish without having the joy of knowing the Lord Jesus.

As I interacted with more and more people from all segments of society, I could sense within myself a growing burden for the poor. Although we lived very simply by Western standards—we had no phone or air conditioning and just enough electricity to run a hair dryer if we turned everything else off—the gap between the poor and me seemed so great. The spiritual gap was greater still. How could I become a clear channel of God's love in a radically different culture? What were the big questions that they struggled with in their lives? I prayed that the Lord would show me how to connect with some of these new friends at a heart level, in ways that would change both my life and theirs.

Ancestral burial plots are very important in the Kantoli culture.

I resolved to continue doing the simple things I'd been doing—making friends, opening my home whenever I could, and responding to the unexpected opportunities that presented themselves. My husband, Steve, was a natural planner, visionary and leader, but I decided I didn't need to have a sophisticated plan. I'd let God reveal His plans for me in His own way and at just the right time.

Back in Denalia, Steve spent a few more years as a student at the university and then got a job teaching English and American culture at a large English academy with several thousand students. Beyond these responsibilities, he started several English schools and was involved in a number of humanitarian and educational projects.

The Kantoli language wasn't easy to learn.

We had a lot of fun researching the Kantoli language and culture with help from students at the university. We conducted detailed surveys in various towns and villages and, in the process, developed wonderful friendships with these bright, young future leaders of the country—and we had many opportunities to talk about spiritual things.

Kantoli dance fascinated me. I was amazed at the beauty and elegance in the dancers' routines. They were slow and graceful, and their costumes glittered with all kinds of colors and designs.

I learned a few of their dances, and they loved it! Soon I was asked to teach English and American culture to a group of top Kantoli dancers who were preparing for a tour of the United States. I hosted a dinner in my home, serving a typical American meal of roast beef, mashed potatoes and peas. It was comical watching them try to balance peas on a fork and swallow mashed potatoes when they had never eaten them before. Everything tasted strange and bland to them. They weren't used to eating food without hot sauce.

The Kantoli dancers were a big hit on their American tour.

The dancers' American tour was a smashing success. They even finished it with a performance for our home church in Pasadena, California. The entire group was hosted in the homes of our church friends for a few days while they toured Los Angeles.

Although these opportunities were exhilarating, I still longed and prayed for something more—for some significant and enduring contribution I could make to the people I had grown to love.

It was around that time that I first met Dewi.

Chapter 4

THE LITTLE VILLAGE WOMAN

- - - - - - - -

*If you help the poor you are
lending to the Lord—and He will repay you!*

—PROVERBS 19:17 NLT

Dewi was from the same area as the Dedeng family, not far
from the town where we had done language research with
the university students. I was somewhat familiar with that
area, having traveled there twice. Like me, Dewi was in her
early twenties—a single mother who moved to the big city hoping to turn her life around. One day she came to my home desperate for work that would help her provide for her baby boy.
She was very small, perhaps four and a half feet tall, and I found
her to be smart, polite and personable.

I had two children, and life was very busy. Our little home
was like Grand Central Station. During our first few years in

Nusandia, we had 140 guests from America, not to mention local guests. Some of them stayed with us for weeks or even months. I could definitely use some help and saw lots of ways to answer Dewi's request.

In Nusandia, it is common practice to hire help around the house. Without washing machines, microwaves and spacious refrigerators, it took a lot of time to do daily household chores. Just to mail a letter at the post office downtown could take two hours. By hiring someone to help us, we could get a lot more done and, at the same time, bless someone with safe and desirable employment.

Dewi, a new friend from an isolated village

I invited Dewi to help me out by shopping for me each day at the local open market and by helping to cook and to babysit Joy and Sarah. She was just what we needed, and Dewi quickly blended into our family. As I got to know her, I found her story to be sadly typical. As a young teenager, Dewi had been given in marriage to a man who had taken her secretly as a second wife. Polygamy is a common practice in most Islamic societies. Often, though, it is done on the sly. A man will have multiple wives in different towns, and each wife may or may not be aware of the others. When Dewi was forced to marry this man, his other wife was not aware of it. When the first wife found out, she pestered her husband until he agreed to divorce Dewi. Dewi's marriage ended as quickly as it had begun, but not before she became pregnant with a baby boy. There was no child support for her; she would have to raise this baby on her own. That is why she fled to the city, desperate for work.

Dewi proved to be faithful and honest. She was a very hard worker and saved me money at the market (Foreigners usually paid more for things if they did their own shopping.) and learned new skills in the kitchen. There was no task that she would not attempt. We talked often of the village where she came from and what her life was like there. I learned much from Dewi about the Kantoli culture and way of thinking. I saw tremendous potential in this young woman whom God had brought across my path. It was no accident, and I knew she was the answer to my prayers in more ways than one.

Dewi had a few other relatives in the city. One day one of them came rushing into our home yelling for Dewi to come quickly. I couldn't understand everything he was saying, but I knew it involved an accident. It sounded very serious. I soon learned that a tragedy had befallen Dewi's nephew, Ade, who worked at the big public swimming pool. That morning his boss had asked for a volunteer to climb some very tall pine trees to trim their branches. Some of the branches were dead, and others were too close to the pool, causing pine needles to fall into the water.

Ade had climbed coconut trees many times, so he volunteered for the job. While others watched from below, he climbed to the top of the first tree carrying a machete with him. As he balanced on a branch sixty or seventy feet up in the air, suddenly the branch gave way, and he fell. To the shock of the crowd standing around and the people swimming in the pool, Ade fell onto the cement pavement. The force of the fall crushed his body and caused some of his bones to burst out of his body. Several bystanders fainted at the horrific sight.

They brought Ade's disfigured body to the one-room shack that Dewi called home. She rushed to see him and console the grieving relatives who had quickly gathered. Dewi was the only one with the presence of mind and emotional stability to make quick decisions.

In Islamic culture, when someone dies, the family tries to bury the body before sunset that same day. Dewi asked if I would be willing to go with her out to her village in Banteng to witness her nephew's burial. Steve and I gave Dewi our van to take the family and the body back to their mountain village. I quickly gathered my things and joined them on the five-hour journey through the mountains. Steve stayed behind to look after Joy and Sarah.

Our van could only go so far before there were no more roads. We got out of the van and hiked up a hill and across the rice paddies, carrying Ade's body. Water buffalo plowed the fields in the distance, and many miles away, I could see a little village hugging the volcanic mountainside as smoke rose from the village houses—some with thatched roofs and others with tin roofs.

When we finally arrived at the village, the sun was sinking behind the mountain ridges. A simple grave had already been dug. There was a brief ceremony, and Ade's body was wrapped in cloth and lowered into the grave. The grave was dug in such a way as to allow space for a response when Allah's angel called the person's name to tell them whether or not they would be allowed into paradise. There were tears, wailing and chanting in Arabic. It was a sad and hopeless event.

The gathered crowd appreciated my presence deeply. As far as anyone could recall, no foreigner had ever been to their little village. Some of these people were seeing a light-skinned person for the first time. As the shadows lengthened and enveloped us in darkness, I longed for a way to help the people of this village. They needed hope.

I returned home late that night totally exhausted. It was hard to process the events of the day. Dewi was back to work the next day, and it helped to ease her mind that she had something else to focus on. I realized how, for most people, life simply continues on as it has for centuries. It's just a matter of surviving from day to day. I sensed that Dewi was weighing the futility of life in her heart. When it seemed appropriate, I talked with her about Christ's victory over death and His love for her and the Kantoli people. She listened quietly and nodded. I wasn't sure how much she understood.

Dewi's village hugged the mountainside.

In the months following, I noticed that there was warmth and responsiveness in the hearts of the new friends I was making in Dewi's family. They were not so shy around me but were comfortable coming to visit in our home. Dewi and the others seemed extremely grateful for the help we'd given in their time of need.

When the next invitation came from Dewi to visit her village, I knew it was a real expression of friendship. This time it would be a happy visit rather than a sorrowful one. Although it required traveling quite a long distance from my home in hot, smoky public transport along bumpy dirt roads, I knew it would be worth the journey. I packed a few things, Dewi and I purchased some treats in the city that were not available in the village and off we went.

The rice paddies in Dewi's home village were a challenge to navigate.

The distance and the winding roads around the mountains struck me again. There was so much twisting and turning. Once again we were dropped off at the edge of a mountain and started the muddy trek upward. This time I was more aware of my surroundings. I saw what looked like yellow dots along the mountainside where the rice terraces came down the slopes like sculpted steps carpeted in shades of green, yellow and brown. I knew what they were: the rice hats of hundreds of people working in the rice paddies. It was harvest time, and everyone was involved.

Here I was in a part of the world that had no contact with the gospel. In my heart, I spoke to the Lord as we continued our hike. "These people seem too many to number," I said. "The task seems impossible."

"Arlene, I know each of them by name." I felt like I'd heard an almost-audible response. "They are not hidden from Me. I love them and paid a very high price to show them My love."

The Bible says, "Even the very hairs on their heads are numbered" (Matt. 10:30). That is how much God cares about each of the individuals living in these hidden valleys.

But what could *I* do to help these people? God was stitching the threads of my heart to theirs. I enjoyed my visit to Dewi's village immensely. The program included her nephew's circumcision celebration, which according to custom is at five or six years of age. For the Kantoli, circumcision is a huge rite of passage, not just for the boys but often for the girls as well. There was a lot of music, dancing and eating, and even a small parade through the village. Dewi's father took me from door to door to meet everyone including a relative who claimed to be 103 years old. He was proud to take me on a tour of the village and did not want me to miss a single detail.

I was taking it all in. I saw where they harvested kidney beans as a source of protein. I saw the stalls that Dewi had built for the goats that she was breeding. I saw big cages of guinea pigs that also helped to feed the village. Dewi herself had started many of these projects. With the wage that I gave her, she was investing in these animals. For villagers, animals meant money, food and security. Frequently, Dewi would give a guinea pig for a meal to a needy person. Dewi had a lot of animals, and she instructed her family how to care for them while she was away in the city. She would compensate those who cared for her animals while she was gone.

With some of her income, she fixed the leaky roof of a small wooden home she had built for her extended family. Although unmarried, she felt a sense of responsibility for her mother, father and siblings. She had only a third-grade education, but she was smart in business and wise with her money. I could see that she was industrious, fair and honest in her dealings with everyone. People came to her with their questions. This little lady friend of mine was obviously respected by her community.

Life in her village was quite different from life in the big city. When I needed to use the restroom, Dewi found an umbrella and led me into the fields behind her home. There was the restroom: a couple of planks across a ditch. Privacy is not a high priority in village culture. I was learning so much, and I was glad to be there in spite of the inconveniences.

Dewi's family welcomed me with a big feast.

That afternoon Dewi's relatives slaughtered a goat in my honor. I knew how valuable that goat was to them, and I felt both honored and guilty that they were butchering it on my account. We made goat satay from every part of the animal, served, of course, with rice. It was a festive occasion with lots of people gathered around,

64

and every one of them was watching me. By this time, I already knew Nusandian and was beginning my study of Kantoli. My language learning process was in high gear here because many of these people didn't speak Nusandian at all—only Kantoli.

Dewi's family members welcomed me with open arms. Not only had I joined them in their time of sorrow, but I had also joined them in a time of celebration. I had braved the long bus ride, the trek into the village, and the exotic food. Most importantly, I was making every effort to speak to them in their own Kantoli language. They loved every minute of it. I was not fluent by any means, but the words that came out of my mouth flowed and were eagerly received with roars of clapping and delight. Once again, the small effort that I was making was going a long way. I realized again how important it is to speak to people in their heart language.

During one of my walks in the village, I met a little girl with bleeding, infected ulcers up and down her legs. One ulcer was especially big, and I was concerned because it looked so infected. I spoke with her mother and asked if I might do something to help this precious little girl. Although she was shy, I could tell by the look in her eyes that she was suffering from these sores. Her parents agreed that I could pray for her and take her back to Denalia for medical treatment.

The family had no money to provide for a doctor's visit or medicine. They were overwhelmed with gratitude for my help. I determined I would take this little girl to my good friend, Dr. Irma. The family went back to their small home and prepared a little bag of personal items for their daughter to take to the city. We would leave in the morning.

I went to bed that night on a grass mat on the wooden floor. The nearby fire warmed the cold mountain air. Some of Dewi's relatives remained up a long time, whispering quietly among themselves. Their cigarettes glowed in the darkness. Dewi's father sat nearby, a self-appointed sentinel in the shadows. All night he watched over us as we slept.

Actually, I wasn't sleeping a whole lot. I had too much to think about. I was grateful to God for the events of that day. God had given me the privilege of being one of the first outsiders to visit this place. What was the responsibility that came with that? In the darkness I prayed, "Lord, allow me to make an impact here. Please, Lord, show me how. Surprise me. I want to be a blessing to these people."

In the quietness I felt I heard an answer: "Arlene, just keep on loving them. I'll take care of the rest. My love will find a way."

I felt a peace come over me. Then the words of a familiar chorus drifted into my mind. We used to sing it a lot in the car as children. Dad and Mom would spontaneously start singing, and we kids would join in:

> *When we walk with the Lord in the light of His Word*
> *What a glory He shines on the way!*
> *While we do His good will, He abides with us still*
> *And with all who will trust and obey.*
>
> *Trust and obey, for there's no other way*
> *To be happy in Jesus, but to trust and obey.*
> *Then in fellowship sweet we will sit at His feet*
>
> *Or we'll walk by His side on the way.*
> *What He says we will do, where He sends we will go.*
> *Never fear, only trust and obey.*

In the morning, Dewi and I left with the little girl and bags of Kantoli snacks showered on us by the villagers. As soon as we got back to Denalia, I didn't waste any time and took the little girl immediately to Dr. Irma. She was surprised that I kept bringing people her way and paying their expenses. The expenses seemed so small, so affordable, compared to health care in the United States. It was a delight to have a small part in improving someone's life simply because I had a few extra dollars.

It was clear to me that my friendship with Dr. Irma was not an accident. God had put me in her path to help the people with their illnesses and to also be an encouragement and example to her. Irma had medical skills I didn't have. We made a great team.

Dr. Irma tested the little girl and concluded that she was allergic to fish. This, combined with the unsanitary conditions in the villages, was causing her wounds to be terribly infected. With some antibiotics, her sores could be healed, but she had to stop eating fish. This was a hard thing to do because the Kantoli diet consists of lots of dried salty fish from their dirty community ponds, but sure enough, after the treatment and as she stayed away from eating fish, the little girl improved dramatically.

Three years had passed since our arrival in Nusandia. We'd left for Asia as a young husband and wife team. Now there were four of us. It was time for our first visit back to the United States. While in the States, we travelled thousands of miles, visiting friends and partners. One day when we were with my parents in Virginia, I climbed up into the attic to look through some boxes I had left there for safekeeping. Rummaging around in the semi-darkness, I discovered a box I had placed there in 1982, shortly after my Grandma Fletcher had died. The box was filled with scraps of cloth that I'd found in her antique shop after the funeral.

As I opened the box, memories flooded my mind.

PART TWO

Chapter 5

LIFE LESSONS

- - - - - - - -

Oh God, you have taught me from my earliest childhood,
and I have constantly told others about
the wonderful things you do.

—PSALM 71:17 NLT

My Grandmother Close was born in 1901 in McKeesport, Pennsylvania, about eight miles from Pittsburgh. One of 13 children, Grandma left school early and lied about her age to get a job in a steel factory when she was just 14 years old. We affectionately called her "B" because my older sister Ginny had difficulty saying "grandma" when she was learning to talk. Growing up, I could sense she'd had a hard life. B was industrious and good with her hands. She loved to cook, knit and sew, and she even taught me how to sew my own clothing. I loved spending time with her.

We gave Grandpa Close the nickname Papap. He was fun loving and gregarious. His family had emigrated from Scotland in the late 1800s. Papap was a personnel director for mine safety in the thriving coal industry of the area. During the Great Depression and World War II, Papap experienced many hardships.

Their fourth child was a darling redhead named Margaret (better known as Peggy), born on March 15, 1933, during the Depression. She was my mother. Growing up, she attended church and even sang in the choir. She became familiar with the religious vocabulary and blended in, although no one ever challenged her about having a personal relationship with Jesus Christ.

Grandma B loved our visits.

My mother first encountered a missionary when her aunts introduced her to a woman who had dedicated her life to serving God in India. This woman's sari, her long ponytail and her mastery of a foreign language amazed my mother. Later Mom heard that this woman had died in India. It made a deep impression on her. These aunts and their missionary friend were the first genuine Christians my mother remembered meeting.

After retirement, Papap spent a lot of time in his woodshop in the cellar. He, too, loved working with his hands. He would call us grandkids down to see his latest creation. Then he would mount it on the wall next to dozens of earlier projects. His creative work was fascinating. His crafts were an expression of his personality and humor.

When Grandma B would put me to bed, she would say a quick prayer: "Now I lay me down to sleep, I pray the Lord my soul to keep. If I should die before I wake, I pray the Lord my soul to take."

Her simple, memorized prayer made me wonder, *Wouldn't it be better to talk to God directly? Wasn't He a real person?* If people talked to me like that, saying the same things every time they saw me, I'd think they were strange. I noticed that B's prayers seemed different than my parents' prayers. Dad and Mom talked to God as if he was a friend.

Sometimes Papap drank a bit too much. Occasionally, I would lie awake and listen to my parents talk with him in the next room. They spoke to him about his life and eternal destiny. My dad was gracious but not afraid to talk about the Bible and spiritual things.

We loved spending time with both my mother's family and my father's family. Though similar in some ways, they were also a study in contrasts.

Grandpa Fletcher was from Morganfield, Kentucky, in the Deep South. He was named Orville because he was born around the time of Orville Wright's first flight. He and Grandma grew up in farming communities. After they married, they moved to Ohio in the 1930s. Grandpa eventually became a trainmaster for the Baltimore and Ohio Railroad in Punxsutawney, Pennsylvania.

In personality, Grandma Fletcher was Grandpa's opposite. Grandma adored Grandpa. He, in turn, let Grandma be herself. She loved people, antiques and business. With seven children,

71

she was not a pampering kind of mother. She taught the kids how to work—and work hard. Because she had all her children organized and under control, she was able to enjoy time spent on her hobbies. She loved purchasing antiques and refinishing them. She purchased part of an old train depot near where Grandpa worked, opened a store and filled it with all kinds of interesting antiques. Her vivacious personality brought people into the shop not only to purchase antiques but because they had a great friend in Grandma. She brightened up everyone's lives and made them laugh.

I have been told that Grandpa Fletcher spent hours on his knees praying for his children, grandchildren and generations to come. He was an incredible family man who loved God and was deeply respected in the community. He died when I was only four years old. My dad said that, in his final hours, Grandpa kept pointing to something in the corner of the room of the hospital. Grandpa said there was something there, though no one else could see it. My father told me that perhaps an angel was waiting there to escort Grandpa to his heavenly home.

After Grandpa died, Grandma devoted herself to her children and her antique shop. She kept Grandpa's photo on her bedside table and spoke fondly of him all the time. Our visits to Grandma's house were some of my strongest and most positive childhood memories. While other grandmothers were knitting or crocheting, mine was refinishing furniture or polishing a silver set that she had just purchased at an auction. Her clothing was stained with furniture polish, and her long auburn hair was tied up in a bun to keep it from interfering with her current project. Grandma was feisty, fun and totally herself.

Grandma didn't let us grandkids sit around like "sick cats," as she put it. She couldn't stand it when someone was idle or bored. There was so much to do and so much of life to experience. She quickly gave people jobs to do and clarified wages up front. Older grandsons groaned as they rearranged huge pieces of antique furniture, shifted large picture frames or hauled boxes of antiques back and forth from the basement. She delighted in mobilizing us all to work.

Granddaughters, too, had to get their hands dirty by moving things, polishing or cooking. There was no place for "sissies" in the Fletcher family. Once I spent the entire day cleaning the kitchen. I could hardly move because it was small and cluttered. Pots and pans were everywhere. Grandma was busy, and antiques took priority over a clean kitchen. I scrubbed until my hands were raw, but somehow it felt good to see the kitchen transformed, even if I knew it would be messy again the next day.

Grandma Fletcher outside her home

One day Grandma sent us grandkids to buy groceries for the family. She made a list and calculated the total cost. She knew the current price for every single item—eggs, milk and flour. My cousins and I walked to the corner grocery and carefully picked out the items. When we realized we were a few pennies short, the lady at the register noticed our embarrassment.

"Are you Virginia Fletcher's grandchildren?" she asked with a smile. When we told her we were, she burst out laughing and let us go. Everyone knew Grandma. She was well loved. When we arrived home, we told Grandma she was a few pennies short in her calculations. She said the eggs must have gone up in price, and she didn't know it!

Sometimes Grandma would send us to the local bakery at the end of the day to buy all the half-priced breads and pastries. This was a huge treat. We would carry them home in big plastic bags and freeze them. This was how she taught us to look for deals and save money. We learned to "buy up opportunities" while they were hot. For another treat, Grandma would buy huge wooden cases of soda pop. She often commented how Coca-Cola used to cost only five cents when she was raising her family!

The wages she paid us for our help were not high, but we were learning important life lessons. If we didn't work hard, we got kicked in the pants! At the end of the day, there would be some reward, like a walk to the local ice cream shop to get a dilly bar or a bottle of soda. I can remember Grandma looking me straight in the eye and asking me to account for what I had done that day. Had I been a strong worker, worthy of a good wage, or had I been slothful? I was nervous to give an account of what I had done and fidgeted in my seat. Then Grandma would burst out in laughter and commend me for the clean kitchen or diligence in moving antiques. But tomorrow was a new day, and Grandma would say, "You are only as good as your last picture. Get moving!"

There were not many places to sleep in Grandma's crowded house. Her downstairs was a show room, packed full of antiques. Sometimes we didn't have a place to sit. Grandma said that was good because we weren't supposed to be sitting anyway. Even the bathroom door would not close completely because there was an antique in the way!

Upstairs there were rooms filled with more antiques and a few beds. Frequently, we were all in the same room. It was difficult to sleep, but fun. Someone would crack a joke and the whole room would shake with laughter. Once we started laughing, it was hard to stop. In the mornings, no one could take showers because Grandma had plants in the bathtub or more antiques. The only place to bathe was in her bathroom downstairs. Even then, it was only a trickle of water because the plumbing was so old. No one complained, not wanting to be labeled a sissy.

Another thing we could not complain about was Grandma's food. She would concoct huge pots of who-knows-what. Grandma would toss all kinds of leftovers into one big stew and call it "supreme." Sometimes I would gag and wonder what I was eating. It was my first lesson on how to be thankful and how not to be a picky eater. It was a lesson that would prove helpful later in my life.

Grandma always saved money and cut costs so that she could purchase more antiques. She could sell anything, even something that looked like junk to me. She had a keen sense for business, more than any one I had ever known. Even though she was so frugal, she was incredibly generous. It brought her great delight to save money and then give it to a great cause. Years later, she gave money so that my parents could visit mainland China. She helped support their work. Grandma said that, of all the cultures she admired, the Chinese were at the top of the list because they were industrious enough to build the Great Wall.

The Fletcher family loved God and country. Grandma was an eternal optimist, and her home was full of laughter, legendary practical jokes and the richness of deep relationships. This must have been what my mother was drawn to when she met and

75

married my dad. She loved the Fletchers, and they embraced her as one of their own. Some of my favorite memories as a child involved listening to my father and his siblings talk about all the practical jokes they had played on each other over the years. Their stories had long shelf lives. They never tired of repeating them. Each time, it seemed, the stories got funnier and funnier.

Chapter 6

IMPORTANT DECISIONS

Only ask, and I will give you the nations as your
inheritance, the ends of the earth as your possession.

—PSALM 2:8 NLT

Born December 1, 1931, my father, Ted, was Grandpa and Grandma Fletcher's third child. He was 19 years old when the Korean War broke out. He had always been drawn to Marine Corps posters that called for "a few good men." Patriotic and adventurous, the thought of serving his country had tremendous appeal. He enlisted in August 1951 and soon found himself on the front lines with the reconnaissance division of the Marine Corps. He was the first to volunteer for dangerous missions behind enemy lines. Many times he risked his own life to drag wounded comrades back to safety. Many of them never made it home.

One day in Korea, a young evangelist named Billy Graham visited the Marines on the front lines. When Dad heard Billy Graham was coming, he could hardly wait to hear him. Dad had always had an interest in spiritual things because of his parents' respect for God and His Word. He had already witnessed the deaths of some of his buddies in the war, and thoughts of eternity were on his mind. Was he next? Was he ready? When Billy Graham concluded his brief message, he gave an invitation to the gathered Marines to accept Jesus as their personal Lord and Savior. My father was one of the first to step forward.

Dad's life was changed on the front lines in Korea.

Shortly after his return from Korea, Dad's siblings fixed him up on a blind date with a beautiful redheaded schoolteacher named Peggy Close (He had always wanted to marry a redhead). At the time, she was dating a young man from church, but that didn't stop my father from asking her on a date. They had both graduated from the University of Pittsburgh; he had a degree in business, and she had a degree in education. He won her heart from day one, and the young schoolteacher went home that night and told her best friend that one day she would marry Ted Fletcher. Dad was equally convinced about her.

They were married in 1956 and moved to Richmond, Virginia, where Dad had landed a promising job with Mobil Oil Company managing several gas stations. He was energetic and excited about the future. He grew rapidly in his faith, spending hours in the word. Mom, on the other hand, while thankful to start a new chapter in her life, found herself struggling with depression.

Dad, as a young businessman

My sister Ginny was born in 1956 and my brother John in 1958. When Mom was a few months pregnant with her third baby, she came down with a serious case of chicken pox. There was hardly a place on her body that did not have a red, itchy mark on it. Daddy was on a business trip, and our family doctor made a house call to look at mom. After examining her, he announced there wasn't much chance she'd have a normal child. He gave Mom a laundry list of the ways that the chicken pox virus can affect an unborn child: blindness, deafness, malformed limbs or no limbs at all.

The doctor suggested Mom might want to consider an abortion. My mother told him she was not interested in aborting her baby. Even so, the exchange fueled the emotional turmoil in her heart. Questions flooded her mind. Could she handle a disabled child at a time when she felt so inadequate?

I was Mom and Dad's third child.

One evening a short time later, Dad opened his Bible to read at the kitchen table, as he often liked to do. He had such peace and seemed to be confident about his eternal destiny. Just as importantly, he was enthusiastic about his life on earth—something Mom sensed was lacking in herself. Feeling caught in a downward spiral and without any answers, Mom turned to Dad and asked him to explain once again how a person could experience this kind of peace and freedom. He took his Bible and opened it to passages in Scripture that spoke of salvation as a free gift from God—not something people could earn by their own efforts.

"The Lord Jesus gave His own life as a sacrifice to pay the price for your sin," he explained, "so that you can live a victorious life and enjoy eternity with Him. All you have to do, Peggy, is simply acknowledge your reliance on God and accept His wonderful gift of salvation."

Mom had heard these things before, but this time it was different. Her heart melted with a realization that these words were truer than she'd ever realized and that she needed a Savior. She bowed her head and, with Dad's encouragement, invited Jesus to take over her life. Then, together, she and Dad committed their unborn child to God's care. They asked Him to spare the baby's life and to bring something beautiful out of the crisis.

On September 9, 1960, I was born—a healthy little baby girl. The doctor said it was an absolute miracle. As Mom watched me grow, I was a constant reminder to her of God's amazing grace.

My mother's life changed noticeably. A growing confidence and peace replaced her prior withdrawal. Instead of watching television alone, Mom started engaging more with people and meeting their needs. She was truly "born again" just like the Bible describes.

After Mom's spiritual rebirth, Dad settled the whole family into Immanuel Baptist Church, a Bible-teaching church in Richmond. Relatively new in their faith, Dad and Mom were excited to learn as much as they could. What was God's big picture? Where was history heading? The first Sunday Dad walked into the foyer of their new church, he saw a huge world map highlighting pictures of missionaries and their locations around the world. The map fascinated him. He had been in Korea as a Marine, but he wondered what it might be like to volunteer for another kind of risky mission, this time for the purpose of taking a life-saving message to the ends of the earth.

81

Pastor Richard Seume saw a lot of potential in Dad and took him under his wing and mentored him. It was a friendship that made an indelible mark on Dad's life and on our whole family. Dad was like a sponge, ready and waiting to do God's will—whenever, wherever and at whatever cost. He was a Marine, but this time, he was responding to God's call. Mom, too, was influenced by what she was learning.

Peggy with Arlene, Ginny, Carol and John

The church had frequent conferences during which missionaries would share their stories and reports. The missionaries often needed a place to stay, a hot meal and a listening ear. Mom and Dad were always the first to open their home and offer accommodations for these honored visitors from distant countries. The conversations over our meal table were absolutely fascinating to my young ears—stories of danger, miraculous provision and answered prayer. It seemed as though the Bible was still being written in the lives of these amazing people. They became heroes to me and my siblings. Our eyes were constantly being lifted off ourselves and beyond our four walls to a world of adventure and need. The four children—by this time Carol had joined us—were rapidly becoming "global Christians."

As they became personal friends with more and more missionaries, my parents began to contribute to the financial needs of some. These missionaries were not guaranteed a monthly paycheck. They relied on the faithful giving of God's people to meet their daily needs and carry out their ministries. Dad and Mom would mention these needs to us around the dinner table, and we talked about ways we could all be involved. Sometimes they would let a missionary family borrow one of our cars for weeks at a time. Dad would give his credit card to a missionary and tell them to go out and buy new clothes for the whole family.

We thought of missionaries as royalty—God's ambassadors. They deserved the very best. Mom and Dad believed not only in tithing their income, but in giving generously, above and beyond the call of duty. They taught us children how to tithe, too. I remember collecting coins in a jar to purchase a new Bible for a single missionary named Mary Baker who lived in Africa. Miss Baker's Bible had fallen into a river when she was traveling by canoe, and we wanted to help her get a new one. Projects like this animated our family. They transported us to distant lands to be a part of a bigger picture than we saw in our suburban Richmond community.

One day we packed a huge metal barrel for a missionary family named the Gregorys. The Gregory family worked among the Asmat tribe on the south coast of New Guinea, just north of Australia. They had four children who were the same ages as we were. I put my favorite doll in the drum for Susan Gregory, and we shipped the barrel to New Guinea. It was really hard for me, but I was learning important lessons of life.

Later the Gregorys spent several weeks at a time living in our home when they were in the U.S. between field assignments. During high school, their oldest daughter lived with us, attending school with my older sister and brother. Hearing daring stories from these missionary children excited me. It created a longing in my heart to experience the world. They certainly were not children who were deprived, as some might think. Their lives were full of adventure as they were part of their parents' team bringing the gospel to a culture still living in stone-age conditions.

Our family also began to pray regularly for missionaries. Our kitchen refrigerator became a prayer depot, with pictures of families working all over the world. The pictures reminded us to back up these people with prayer. The four of us children watched the growth of a world vision right within our own home. Although Dad and Mom might not have realized it, we weren't missing a thing. My parents brought the world to our dinner table in conversation, to our living room as we assembled care packages for those living on other continents and to our bedrooms as we prayed for individuals each night before drifting off to sleep. These prayers were very meaningful to me, and I felt like I was making a difference in their lives and in the world. We were small, but God was planting seeds that would grow strong through the years.

We didn't know it at the time, but Dad and Mom were praying their own serious prayers regarding their personal involvement in God's global cause. In his reading, Dad came across Psalm 2:8: "Only ask, and I will give you the nations as your inheritance, the ends of the earth as your possession."

Daddy's heart and mind were riveted on that verse. He took God's promise as applying not only to the Lord Jesus, but also in a personal way to himself. Increasingly, my father felt that this ancient promise would be fulfilled, in part, through our family. Dad and Mom prayed that they would somehow have the privilege of going to a distant country as well. More than that, they prayed that their four children would all have that opportunity. Often Dad would spontaneously turn to us and quote William Carey: "If God calls you to be a missionary, don't stoop to be a king."

Chapter 7

THE PAGES OF
YOUR LIFE

- - - - - - - -

We spend our years as a story that is told. So teach us
to number our days, that we may apply our hearts unto wisdom.

–Psalm 90:9, 12 KJV

I was Ted and Peggy Fletcher's third child. Ginny, who is four years older than I am, was confident, capable and in charge. John, like his Grandpa Fletcher, was the ultimate gentleman, quiet and deeply thoughtful. Carol, my younger sister, completed the family with her beautiful singing voice and mischievous sense of humor.

I, on the other hand, was seriously shy and often felt like the new kid in school—which I usually was. Because Dad was energetic and successful, he was frequently promoted or transferred to other parts of the country. After several years with Mobil Oil, he accepted a new role in sales with *The Wall Street Journal*. Through the years, we moved to New York, New Jersey, Michigan, Maryland, California and on and on. We lived in nearly 20 different homes before I turned 20. While I was in the sixth grade, for example, I went to three different schools—two on the east coast and one on the west coast!

The frequent moves were not always easy. From our many moves, I learned that parents and siblings are a young girl's most important friends. My mother was a teacher by training, so she helped us navigate all the transitions.

Me at age 10—change was a part of life.

One day when I was attending kindergarten in Rockville, Maryland, I didn't show up at the bus stop after school. Every bus stop looked the same to me, and I became confused. When I was still on the bus after the last stop, the driver asked if I was lost. I replied, "Yes," and he circled around the entire bus route again until I finally figured out where I was supposed to get off. Imagine how concerned my mother was when I finally showed up! It was not the last time that I would become lost in a new environment from our constant moves.

From Maryland we went to Buffalo, New York, where I entered the first grade. Once again, seriously shy, I had to survive in a harsh world. I was laughed at because of my long, curly auburn hair. An insensitive teacher made the year even harder for me. During art lesson one day, we were told to color a picture of strawberries. The teacher came up behind me and hovered over my shoulder. Suddenly, I got a swift whack on my little hand. She told me that I was messy and shouldn't have colored outside the lines. I was shocked and couldn't hold back my tears. Eventually, she sent me to stand in the corner of the room. I couldn't stop crying, and finally the teacher called in my older sister, Ginny, to comfort me.

Later that year my teacher wrote on the bottom of my report card, "Arlene is a problem child." I studied my father's face as he read the report, anxious to see how he would respond. He put the letter down, looked at me and broke into a big smile. Then, picking me up in a giant bear hug, he began to laugh and laugh.

Dad thought it was so funny because, to him, I was such an easy, compliant child. He saved that report card all through the years in a box of memories. It was a great reminder to him of how wrong people could be. From time to time, he would remind me to deliberately "color outside the lines." "It's good to be different," he'd tell me. In his mind, going against the flow was a positive characteristic—something he applauded.

In time, I learned to be tougher and not let people push me around. Dad and Mom helped me a lot. Sometimes they would give me a small stack of gospel tracks to give to my teachers and classmates. This taught me courage. No one was too young to share the good news, Dad told us.

I learned how important it is to not let any opportunity pass and not to be intimidated by those who are antagonistic toward the message of Christ—even if they are authority figures. My responsibility was to be faithful in sharing the Good News.

And I learned creative ways to do this through my brother, John. When he was 15 years old, John bought an answering machine, and each day he would record a new dial-a-message Bible reflection. We passed out cards at school with the phone number on them, and John would follow up with each person who called in to leave a voice recording. A newspaper in New Jersey, where we were living at the time, even wrote an article about John, calling him "a future Billy Graham." He started a group called Youth Aflame and would have large gatherings of students at our home. We took the high school by storm and soon outgrew the library room. The principal's two sons, for example, were atheists. They both came to faith in Christ through the influence of my brother and another friend. One of them went on to become a pastor. We went through the yearbook and made sure everyone had an opportunity to hear about the Lord.

Dad was a fast-rising executive at *The Wall Street Journal* and eventually became the national sales manager. Dad loved sales and the WSJ and found many ministry opportunities there as he led co-workers to Christ. The job also provided us the opportunity to give substantial financial support for several missionary families. Yet in spite of all the good things about his job, Dad felt God had something else for him in the future. The Lord had planted in his heart a growing desire to be more directly involved in what God was doing in the world beyond American borders.

A good friend challenged my Dad: "Your life is like a book, Ted. What are you writing on the pages of your life?"

Dad never forgot this. He often quoted Psalm 90:9,12: "We spend our years as a story that is told, so teach us to number our days that we might apply our hearts to wisdom." Dad constantly evaluated his life in terms of eternity. As much as he loved the business world, he sensed that he would not spend all of his remaining years in that environment.

Dad and Mom tested the waters by applying to various mission organizations to see if they could use some help. With Dad's background in business, he and Mom thought there might be a place for them to serve overseas. The answers varied but always boiled down to the same conclusion: "You don't have any formal theological training. You haven't had any mission experience. You have four children. You need this. You need that."

It seemed that having a desire to spread the gospel among the nations and the experience of being national sales manager for a world-renowned corporation weren't enough. *It shouldn't be so hard to get involved*, Dad thought. Through the years, Dad kept a notebook of rejection letters from the various agencies he contacted. This didn't discourage him, though. It only fueled his desire to find a way to make an impact on the world.

As Dad and Mom considered their options, they talked with another close friend from New Zealand, Dr. William Miller, who was a mobilizer at heart and had always encouraged Dad not to give up his dream. This time, however, his words went beyond encouragement as he asked a penetrating question that changed my Dad's life: "Ted, why don't you start your own mission agency?"

It wasn't long after that when Dad made his final decision to leave the *Journal*. He talked with the family regarding his desire to explore new opportunities to serve the Lord. We were not surprised because we'd seen it coming. It was not a matter of *if* Dad would leave but *when*.

As a family, we were excited to live by faith and trust God for all of our needs. I was a sophomore in high school, and it was difficult for me to leave behind my cheerleading (Yes, I was learning to be less shy) and youth group. We moved to northern Virginia to be part of my Uncle John's church, Faith Bible Church. Dad started a one-truck moving company to put groceries on the table. He used the remainder of his time to volunteer at a Christian college. We were there for two years before Dad accepted a job with Gospel Light Publications in Glendale, California. John and Ginny were in college in Maryland, but Carol and I relocated to California with Dad and Mom.

I was 16 years old, and on that long drive, I read aloud to my parents and Carol from a best-selling book by Don Richardson, which my brother John had given me before we left. In fact, he loved it so much that he insisted everyone in the family read it. *Peace Child* was the riveting story of the Richardson family's 15-year adventure as missionaries in the jungles of New Guinea. Many of the tribes living in the remote jungles of this island were headhunters, even cannibals. Few had experienced any meaningful contact with the outside world.

Don and Carol Richardson in a dugout piloted by Sawis

Most people would be terrified of traveling halfway around the world to reach out to people like this, but for Don and his wife, Carol, these tribes were like a powerful long-distance magnet that drew them across the Pacific. Don was born on Prince Edward Island in eastern Canada. At age 10, shortly before his father's death from cancer, Don and his family moved to Victoria, a picturesque town nestled on the southern end of Vancouver Island. Carol's parents had served churches in the Ozarks, Oklahoma, Winnipeg and now Cincinnati. They met at Prairie Bible Institute on the snow-swept plains of central Alberta, and despite strict school rules, their romance blossomed. They married in August 1960, and just two years later, the young family—now including a son named Stephen—began a journey to the other side of the world.

As my own family drove across the country, we were mesmerized by the Richardsons' adventures. It took two months for them to get to their new home. On the final stretch, they paddled their way through the headwaters of the Kronkel River into the jungle domain of a stone-age tribe called the Sawi. The Sawi were located 40 river miles inland from the spot on the south coast where Michael Rockefeller had vanished in October, 1961. Michael was son of Nelson Rockefeller, who was governor of New York and became the 41st Vice President of the United States. Michael had been collecting primitive art from the Asmat, a warrior tribe whose territory bordered the Sawi.

I loved reading about the Sawi, who were tree dwellers, whose houses swayed 30 or 40 feet above the swamp, like giant loaves of bread caught in the trees. They decorated their walls and fireplaces with bird feathers—along with the skulls of dead loved ones and slain enemies. Warfare was a way of life. It was clan against clan, village against village, tribe against tribe. Add crocodiles, death adders and clouds of malarial mosquitoes to the mix, and it is nothing short of a miracle that tribes like the Sawi had survived.

My family and I marveled that a happily married young couple in their mid-20s would choose cannibals for neighbors and a hut on stilts with see-through walls as their first home. *How, we wondered, would their son play in parasite-infested swamps?* We pictured him navigating the jungle trails like a modern-day Tarzan, munching on sago grubs, termites and cassowary eggs. He must have seemed strangely out of place, the little blond haired boy who wore nothing but shorts, chattering effortlessly with Sawi friends and paddling his stand-up sports canoe through tea-colored rivers.

Steve with one of his Sawi playmates

Images like these danced through my mind as I read *Peace Child* that summer of 1977. I could see why my brother, John, loved the book, as John himself was sensing a call to a tribal group similar to the Sawi. He wanted to translate the Bible into a tribal language. The Richardsons' amazing story impacted me in a similar way. I found myself transported to a distant world. My heart was captivated with the notion that I too could be God's ambassador to a radically different culture, learn an exotic language and grow to love the ways of the people. I could see myself transforming a thatch-roofed shelter into a simple home, treating tropical infections and diseases, delivering babies by firelight, teaching men, women and children to read God's Word, and raising my family among them. The combination of risk, adventure and spiritual fruitfulness was irresistible.

Suddenly, the careers that my high school friends were considering seemed colorless. As our car traveled west toward California, I wanted to leave New Jersey far behind—and the American dream with it. I had discovered a cause far more compelling. I sensed within my heart a growing determination to live my life on the edge.

Chapter 8

AN ARRANGED MARRIAGE

We can make our plans, but the LORD determines our steps.

–Proverbs 16:9 NLT

We settled into yet another new home—this one in Arcadia, California. Dad began work at Gospel Light Publications in nearby Glendale. One day he came home from work and told us that he had taken an author to lunch: Don Richardson. I was amazed that my father got to meet the author of the book I'd fallen in love with. In fact, Gospel Light had published the book, and Dad explained that Don was writing another book, *Lords of the Earth*, which was due out soon.

I begged Dad to bring home a copy of the manuscript because I couldn't wait to read it. Dad did not disappoint me. The next day he came home with a big stack of paper. It was the true life story of an Australian missionary who was killed by a cannibal tribe in West Papua. A few months later, an airplane crashed into the same mountain valley. A family had been on board, and the only passenger to survive the crash was a ten-year-old boy. I stayed up until two o'clock in the morning reading the typewritten pages, tears streaming down my face. I became very intrigued with New Guinea and began praying for the island. I glued a map of the island into my Bible, and whenever I met missionaries who had lived there, I asked them to sign the map.

In high school, all my heroes were missionaries.

By this time, I was over my shyness, and in high school, I found it kind of fun to be considered a person who went "against the flow." Sure, I was an easterner, but it was more than that. I wasn't all that interested in the usual things that high school girls were interested in. My confidence as a person had grown substantially. I was excited about my faith and made no apologies for it.

That year I dated a handsome, six-foot-four baseball player who was a freshman at Biola University—the kind of guy all the girls swooned over. We had a lot of fun and enjoyed each other's company. Todd was a great friend, but he was headed for the major leagues, and I was headed for the South Pacific.

"All your heroes are missionaries!" Todd protested.

He was a bit skeptical that I would ever follow through on my dreams, crazy as they were. Todd later went on to pitch for the St. Louis Cardinals and the Los Angeles Dodgers.

Though new at the school, I was elected one of four senior princesses at homecoming. Surprisingly, I was also asked to represent our school in the tryouts for Queen of the Rose Bowl parade. This was a big deal in Southern California. As I stood there with the last few contestants, the judges asked me what made me unique. I answered that God had done a lot for me and I wanted to honor Him by making an impact on the world. It was not quite the answer they were looking for.

That year I was selected best-dressed girl for the school yearbook. My mother and I really laughed about that. The picture that the yearbook committee chose showed me in an outfit that cost me only 25 cents. I had rummaged through a second-hand store and found some pink material for a quarter. I took it home, and Mom and I made a skirt and top out of it. We spent a lot of time on the sewing machine, and I made many of my clothes for school. I enjoyed finding old clothes in the Goodwill store and taking them apart to create something new. I felt like I was making something out of nothing. I must have learned something from being around Grandma Fletcher all those years.

In 1978 I graduated from high school and joined my brother, John, and sister Ginny at Washington Bible College (WBC) in

Maryland. I was a family girl, and I wanted to be with my siblings. Besides, I wanted to study the Bible so that I could prepare for missionary service.

Shortly after my departure to college, Dad took the next step in his own journey: He decided to leave the business world completely—not just *The Wall Street Journal,* but also the Christian publishing world. He was on a quest to pursue his life-long dream of direct personal involvement in global missions, and our entire family cheered him on.

Dad and Mom sold their beautiful house in Arcadia and moved back to northern Virginia. Gathering a group of friends around him, Dad launched a mission organization and called it World Evangelical Outreach. The first office was in our basement. Dad and Mom interviewed the first missionaries in our living room. Their vision was based on Romans 15:20, to "preach the Good News where the name of Christ has never been heard," rather than where a church has already been started by someone else. They wanted to help emerging leaders and ministries in the Pacific Islands and Africa. They also had a heart for China which, at the time, was closed to foreigners.

Not everyone shared my father's vision, however. One mission leader rather bluntly asked Dad, "Who would have the audacity to start another mission board?" Another said, "We already have enough mission agencies." A seminary professor thought Dad and Mom had chosen the wrong name and suggested they limit themselves to a small area of the world—not the entire world. "Why don't you call yourselves *Africa* Evangelical Outreach?" he asked.

"Because God has given us the world," Dad responded. God's promise to him was clear once again: "Only ask, and I will give you the nations as your inheritance, the ends of the earth as your possession" (Psalm 2:8 NLT).

It must have seemed crazy to them that a person with no formal theological training was now the self-appointed director of a mission with a global-sounding name, operating out of his own home. Yet Dad and Mom were seeing their new venture through eyes of faith, and thankfully, the Lord kept bringing them others who had similar vision. In the weeks that followed, they shared their plans with every pastor and church who would listen, starting at our own church. Invitations came, doors opened and we were underway.

I was in my first semester at college when I heard that Don Richardson would be the speaker at the coming mission conference. I hoped to get the chance to talk with him and organized a group of students to have lunch with him. I asked him question after question about *Peace Child* and *Lords of the Earth*, which had been published by that time. I couldn't wait to call my parents and tell them that I'd had lunch with Don Richardson, author of my favorite books. Dad knew Don from Gospel Light, of course, and was glad to know he was in our part of the country. He immediately contacted Don and invited him over to our home in northern Virginia, just an hour away, for dinner. He suggested that Don spend the night, and Dad would take him to the airport the next morning.

When I heard about this arrangement, I decided to go home for the weekend, too. I couldn't get enough of Don's stories about life in New Guinea. For the first time, I heard the rest of the story about Steve, their young son who was just a baby in *Peace Child*. Now he was all grown up; a year younger than I am, he was attending high school in Pasadena, California. Surely coming out of the jungle into Los Angeles was not an easy transition for him and his brothers.

The next morning my parents took Don to Dulles Airport to catch his flight to Los Angeles. When they returned home, they both had mischievous smiles on their faces. It seems that Don asked my father if he could initiate contact between his son Steve and me. He thought we might make a great match! Dad said he was surprised but also intrigued by the idea. For the remainder of the drive the two dads joked about being like a couple of Asian parents and arranging a marriage. Don would talk to Steve and ask if he wanted to have a pen-pal relationship with me. All I had to do was wait to see if Steve would write me.

Two weeks later an envelope arrived in the mail. I opened it and pulled out sheets of stationery from the U.S. Center for World Mission's Institute of Tribal Peoples Studies. Each piece of paper was decorated with sketches of war-painted tribal faces—men with bones through their noses. It wasn't the kind of decoration that most girls would find romantic, but Steve had picked exactly the right letterhead for me. I was very interested in working with tribal people and loved it! I reciprocated with a letter of my own.

One day Dad came into my room to tell me that Don Richardson was on the phone and wanted to talk with me. Dad and Mom's mission organization had a summer program for young people, and Don heard that I had signed up to join one of our teams going to Papua New Guinea. He thought I might be passing through the Los Angeles airport and wondered if he and Steve could meet me there. I thought it was a good idea, except for the fact that I was traveling with several other college students, and we had an overnight layover in Los Angeles. Don suggested that the entire team stay in their home that night, and he and Steve would take us to the airport the next day.

I was very excited about the idea but also felt a bit nervous. Our meeting in the LA airport with Steve and his Dad was like a storybook. We felt privileged as a team to meet with a family who had influenced all of us. In fact, *Peace Child* was now required reading in the missions class at our college. Steve drove me from LAX to Pasadena in his car. When we arrived at the house, everyone congregated in the dining room, but Don somehow made sure that Steve and I had an opportunity to talk alone in the living room. It was all quite comical and surreal, but also fun.

Carol, Don, Valerie, Paul, Steve and Shannon Richardson in 1979

Steve was interesting and polite. Our conversations centered on his upbringing in the jungles and transitions to life here in America. I could feel my heart race, wondering if I was talking with the person I would spend the rest of my life with. Would he like me? Would I be a disappointment to him? Was I the kind of person he was looking for? Was he having similar thoughts?

101

Our romantic evening was over in a flash. I left for New Guinea the next morning, hoping that Steve would write to me while I was there. I was assigned to a remote jungle station among a cannibalistic tribe called the Biami. Interestingly enough, this tribe was quite similar to the Sawi people. Once every week or two, a small plane would land on the airstrip, bringing mail and supplies—but there was never a letter from Steve. I tried not to think about what that meant and attempted to focus on our team's work, but it was difficult.

I loved the Biami people of Papua New Guinea.

In New Guinea, I lived with an Australian couple who had their own unique way of doing things. I was privileged to learn from them, though the summer was not easy. We would start each day with a huge bowl of porridge, followed by long hours of physical labor or typing of the Scripture translation. I quickly fell in love with the tribal people. A highlight of my summer was a multi-day trek through the jungle, traveling with Biami to look for a new site for an airstrip. Each night we slept near an open fire to keep the mosquitoes at bay. During the day we hiked trails, climbed over logs and crossed streams. At one point along the trail, we saw a human jawbone hanging from the branch of a tree. One of the Biami men traveling with us looked at the jawbone and said something to me in his Biami language which, of course, I could not understand.

I waited while someone translated and just about fainted when I learned what he said: "I ate that woman." This man, once a cannibal, had killed a woman because she had wandered into the wrong part of the jungle, an area forbidden to women. It was a point of much discussion the rest of the hike as the Biami Christians and the missionary talked to this man about the freedom that can be found in Christ.

I loved my time in Papua New Guinea, and the only real disappointment was that Steve never wrote to me. I returned to WBC and entered my junior year. One day—nine months after I returned home—a very worn letter arrived in the mail for me. It was from Steve. He had addressed it to me in Papua New Guinea while I was there, but somehow, I never got it. Instead it had gone to all the wrong places around the world and was finally forwarded to me at WBC. The envelope was tattered from nine months of international travel! It was a great letter, and I called my parents to read it to them. Although the letter reached me late, my father urged me to reply anyway.

By this time, Steve was studying at Columbia International University in South Carolina. He, too, was preparing for overseas service. Steve received my letter, and he replied, starting a steady flow of correspondence between the two of us. Each letter would fuel our level of interest in each other a little more. It rapidly became a long-distance romance.

Steve first visited me in the fall of 1981. In those days he would drive cross-country from Los Angeles to Columbia, South Carolina, for school each semester. It would take him 60 hours of driving each time because the national speed limit was 55 mph. This time he took a detour via Washington, D.C., so that he could see me. It was about seven o'clock on a Saturday evening when Steve drove through the gate of my college in his little 1974 Honda Civic. He'd driven all the way from Los Angeles. As I went out to meet him, half the girls in our women's dormitory were peeking through their curtains to watch. I was in charge of my floor of the dormitory, and all my friends were excited. Suspense had been building for days. Steve got out of his car and gave me a big hug. I waved goodbye to everyone secretly watching from the dorm windows, got into his little car, and rode with him to my parents' home in northern Virginia.

We arrived about nine o'clock that night, and Dad immediately asked Steve to teach the adult Sunday school class at church the next morning. He wanted to see if Steve could handle pressure and if he could speak publicly. Steve passed the test with flying colors. On Monday I skipped school, and we spent the day visiting various sites around the capital. We toured the Smithsonian and then stopped for a picnic on the lawn in front of the Supreme Court building. There Steve asked if I was feeling the same sense of destiny that he was.

"What do you think of marriage?" he asked me.

I was a bit shocked and replied, "I think it's a good thing."

Steve's confidence and directness surprised me but also attracted me. This was fun! I felt that God was bringing us together in an amazing kind of romance, but neither of us was quite ready. At least it was fun to dream. Everything seemed to fit—our families, our life goals, our values and standards. Even though we still had college and a lot of learning ahead of us, the Lord seemed to be orchestrating the connection.

One day when I was a senior in college in 1982, my mother called me to say that Grandma Fletcher had passed away. A sense of profound sorrow came over the family. Our amazing grandmother had been the head of the family since Grandpa Fletcher had died in 1964.

Me with my mother, Peggy

Everyone gathered for her funeral. Each family member was given an opportunity to choose something from Grandma's antique shop. I could have chosen any heirloom or antique but was drawn instead to an old box of scrap cloth I found in the corner. Why was this here? I thought to myself. Grandma never sewed anything. She was into furniture, frames and silver. Perhaps she got this particular box as part of some furniture deal at an auction.

Regardless of its origin, I chose the box of scrap cloth, thinking I might like to make a quilt. I knew how to sew but didn't know the first thing about making quilts—but maybe I'd learn someday. After the funeral, I brought the box home with me to northern Virginia and put it in Mom and Dad's attic. Little did I know where I would be when I would see that box again.

Chapter 9
TIME FOR A WEDDING

Weeping may go on all night, but joy comes with the morning.

– PSALM 30:5 NLT

Steve and I spent the spring break of 1983 together at my family's home in Washington, D.C. One evening, as we were enjoying dinner together at a beautiful restaurant overlooking the Potomac River, Steve surprised me with a diamond ring. He was a senior in college, and I was working on my master's degree at Columbia International University (CIU). I knew he was exactly the kind of person I'd dreamed of sharing my life with. He was the adventurous visionary I wanted. I am so glad I waited for God to show me the right one. We were filled with high hopes for the future, so we decided to get on with married life and not wait until school was over.

We were married on December 27, 1983, on a snowy northern Virginia night. Our wedding was beautiful. My only regret was that my brother, John, could not be with us for such a special occasion. He was now a missionary in the middle of Papua New Guinea where he was learning the Kubo language. He was fulfilling the vision God had placed on his heart in his early teens.

Friends and family pitched in, and we were able to do the entire wedding, including dress, décor, dinner and a reception for all the guests, for about $1,500. The wedding ceremony had lots of family participation and included many references to Psalm 67, Psalm 145 and other passages that highlight God's love for the world. Our desire to give ourselves to each other and to world missions came through loud and clear.

Me and my father, Ted, on my wedding day

Two of the many friends who came to our wedding were John and Dawn. They too were from CIU and excited about forming a new team with us to go overseas. Dawn's family was one of the families we had prayed for when I was a little girl. Dawn's parents worked among a tribe called the Dani, the largest tribe in West New Guinea's highlands. They were among the first to enter the area. The Dani responded in large numbers to the gospel. Within a few years they sent out hundreds of their own missionaries to help evangelize remaining unreached tribal groups on their own island.

Dawn and Steve had gone to the same boarding school together in New Guinea. It was an honor to have John, Dawn and her younger brother, David Scovill, with us for our special day. David was a close friend of Steve's younger brother, Paul.

After our wedding, Paul and David stayed up until the early hours of the morning. They hadn't seen each other for several years, so there was lots of catching up to do. After breakfast the next morning, Dawn and John picked up David, and they started the long drive back to their home in South Carolina. David read aloud one of the Psalms that was highlighted in our wedding, Psalm 145. The beautiful verses talked about praising the Lord forever and ever. John, Dawn and David paused a moment, and David said he wanted to read it again.

Just as he finished reading it the second time, their car hit a patch of ice, spinning out of control. John tried to maintain control, but an oncoming pick-up truck crashed into the side of their car. David was killed instantly. John was hurt badly from hitting the steering wheel. Dawn, who was in shock but not seriously injured, managed to get out of the car and stagger to a nearby house for help.

Steve and I were oblivious to the tragedy, of course. We were already on our honeymoon, but we had troubles of our own, though they were small in comparison. On our wedding day, Steve wasn't feeling well. During the ceremony, he began to get chills—and not the normal kind you get when you're getting married. The day after our wedding, the chills were coming every four hours, and he knew exactly what it meant. The cold winter weather was triggering a recurrence of malaria, which was in his bloodstream. Steve had malaria often when he was growing up in the tropics. Once it is in your system, it can lie dormant. He had experienced recurrences like this quite often—but this was on his honeymoon! We were supposed to be driving to the New England area, but by evening he was so sick that it was not reasonable to drive anywhere. We stayed at the hotel, and I gave him Chloroquine tablets every four hours.

Steve and I on our wedding day, December 27, 1983

We still didn't know anything about the car accident. We returned from our honeymoon a few days early, and when we walked in the front door of my parent's house, we were met with a room full of somber faces. Steve's brothers, Paul and Shannon, were standing there—and we knew they should have long since returned to California. When my mother told us what happened,

I felt sick inside and could hardly believe my ears. Here was Steve recuperating from malaria, and now one of our friends, the only son of his parents, had died tragically. It was a nightmare.

Many who had attended our wedding now gathered, once again, for the funeral of an outstanding young man. My sister Carol sang, and Paul and Shannon were pallbearers. Who would have thought such tragedy could hit right after the wedding? Why would God allow such a time of celebration and sorrow to be mixed together? We grieved for David's parents and for Dawn and John, our future teammates.

It was a sobering beginning for our new marriage and life together.

A few days later, we returned to Columbia—now with no place to live. The Scovills had planned to return to Papua, and we were going to move into their trailer. But because of their son's death, they postponed their departure. We ended up living with one of our professors for two weeks while we searched for an apartment.

Steve and I were both still finishing our study programs. We had no income and depended on our wedding gifts to pay our rent and put food on the table. We managed to save money by eating a lot of macaroni and cheese, eggs, hot dogs and peanut butter-and-jelly sandwiches. Things continued to be very tight for our first few years. It was stressful, but we learned to live frugally and depend on the Lord.

After one semester, I had finished most of my course work and was able to find a job on the other side of the city typesetting advertisements for a hardware company. We also moved from our expensive apartment into an old modular trailer behind someone's house. This was much better because it cost only $150 per month—although it had its challenges. There was no ductwork under the heat vents in the floor, so the grass grew right up into our little living room and kitchen. Occasionally, we had to "mow the grass" and vacuum at the same time!

The owner promised to install heat before winter came, but somehow, he never got around to it. By the time the cold weather arrived, there was so much frost on the inside of the walls that we could leave handprints on them. Finally, Steve bought a kerosene heater, but one night we must have put the wrong kind of kerosene in it. When we woke up in the morning, everything was black in our bedroom—even our faces. We looked like raccoons!

Steve and I, of course, pondered our future and wondered what God had in store for us. We knew He wanted us to be His ambassadors to a needy group of people, but where did *He* want us to go? It was a big world, and there were so many options and needs. For Steve, returning to a tribal setting would be like going home. It would be easy and make sense in some ways—yet he really wanted a new challenge, perhaps even an urban environment with a large population. We thought of traveling to China to work as English teachers or going somewhere in the Middle East or Turkey. We even had an interest in Central Asia, then part of the Soviet Union, but there was no way for Americans to go there in those days. Then there was the Muslim world, which had such a vast need.

In time, we began to focus our attention on heavily-populated Nusandia. This seemed to be a natural destination for a number of reasons. First, there were some large people groups there, numbering in the millions, with little or no Christian witness. Second, Steve knew some of the Nusandian language from his childhood experience at a boarding school in an area where some Nusandian was spoken. Third, there were several large cities where Islam was the dominant religion.

By this time, the organization my parents had started had been renamed Pioneers and was beginning to expand around the world. We learned that the board of directors had identified the Kantoli of Nusandia as a group needing a missionary team. Although Steve had grown up in Nusandia, he'd been in an isolated, tribal part of the vast island nation, and he had little awareness of larger people groups in more developed parts of the country where there are huge cities with millions of people. We both began to read about the Kantoli—and of course, to pray.

Choosing a people group to work with seemed like a huge commitment, almost like marriage! We would be giving years of our lives to learning their language, mastering their culture and living among them. This decision would shape our entire lives and the lives of our children. It felt overwhelming.

One day Steve was getting his hair cut in the basement of the men's dormitory at the college. A freshman student was sweeping the floor nearby. Steve had heard that this young fellow was a missionary kid from Nusandia. Thinking he might know something about the Kantoli, Steve struck up a conversation. The young man—Mike Casey—not only had heard of the Kantoli, but his parents, Roger and Janice, worked among them almost singlehandedly for decades.

When Steve told me about the encounter, we knew it was not a coincidence. God was giving us direction. Even more strategic, Mike told us that his parents were going to be in the U.S. a few months later. We arranged to visit them, and their stories and insights were tremendously helpful. It seemed as if God was drawing our attention to this group in many different ways. The more we prayed and the more we learned, the more we felt drawn to that part of the world and that particular culture.

Columbia International University was a great place to learn about cross-cultural work. It was also a great place to find teammates. We were with others who were headed in the same direction—people who were passionate about reaching the nations. We sensed the wisdom of an old African proverb: "If you want to go fast, go alone. If you want to go far, go together." We preferred not to go alone. Teams are effective, and this was one of the core values of Pioneers. We prayed that God would form a team for us right there at Columbia, from among our friends.

Like Steve and me, John and Dawn were newlyweds at Columbia. We enjoyed meals with them and started to explore the possibility of forming a team together. Dawn and John had both heard of the Kantoli and were also contemplating work in Nusandia. It was a logical fit. Steve and Dawn had grown up going to the same boarding schools in Nusandia, and both could speak Nusandian, the trade language which unites the thousands of islands and people groups within the country. We decided to plan a survey trip together to Nusandia during the summer of 1984. Our goals were to see the needs firsthand and to determine how we could best secure entrance into the country. What an educational and eye-opening experience! The four of us traveled all over, meeting with various church leaders, asking them about the Kantoli and exploring ways we might be involved long term.

Over and over again, we kept hearing a recurring theme: "The Kantoli are very hard to work with." After a while, we began to look at each other and wonder if we were really ready to embark on such a mission! Even Nusandian Christian leaders thought the Kantoli were "impossible." Several of them had tried themselves and failed. To make matters worse, John and I got very sick from the food we were eating. Dawn and Steve seemed to have stomachs of steel; they were missionary kids who seemed to get away with eating anything they wanted.

In spite of sickness and discouraging words, in the end, the four of us were united in our desire to embrace the challenge of helping to bring the gospel message to the Kantoli people. Our prayer was like that of Joshua's friend Caleb in the Old Testament: "Give us this mountain!" (Joshua 14:12).

Although I had always envisioned myself working with a tribal group in a jungle setting, I felt some relief that we would be going to a densely populated area. The island where the Kantoli live is shaped like the state of Tennessee, long and narrow, yet it is home to more than 120 million people. This was going to be quite an adventure.

First, though, we had to finish graduate school. After our survey trip, we returned home, and Steve and I focused on getting our master's degrees in intercultural studies from Columbia, which we did in 1985. By that time, we had already been through the formal process of joining Pioneers. After graduation, we spent a year based in Pasadena, California, with our home church, Lake Avenue Church. During that time, we visited churches all across the U.S., sharing with them our growing vision for the Kantoli people. Many of these churches committed to pray for us and help with our financial needs. God brought us other sharp young couples who wanted to join in the work, including Larry and Lula and my sister Carol and her husband, Gary.

By May 1986, we were ready. Steve and I were in our early 20s when we boarded our flight in Los Angeles. We had two large suitcases and two small suitcases, containing everything we owned, but our hearts were full of faith and anticipation. The Lord had called us, and He would "make our path straight" (Hebrews 12:13).

PART THREE

Chapter 10

FROM SCRAPS TO QUILTS

- - - - - - - -

The only thing that counts is faith expressing itself through love.

—GALATIANS 5:6

When Dewi and I opened the box of beautiful quilts that the Senders from North Carolina had made out of my grandmother's fabric scraps, Dewi wanted to learn how to make a quilt. I had never made one before, but I thought that together we could learn how. There was certainly plenty of fabric all around us. Denalia was the textile capital of Nusandia, and I had discovered blocks of textile kiosks selling fabric in all colors and sizes. I gave Dewi a little money and suggested she go pick out some cloth and batting. She asked me if she could take the quilts home to her village, to show her friends and relatives.

"Sure, Dewi," I agreed. "See what they think! I'm sure they'll love them."

A week or so later, a group of men from Dewi's village came to my door and asked to see me. They were reserved and very polite. In their hands they held the quilts from the ladies in North Carolina. I invited them inside for some tea. One of the men, Dadang, was Dewi's brother-in-law. He made a living by selling soup on the side of the road. His little one-man business netted less than 25 cents a day. On such a meager income, he struggled to provide for his wife and five children. I knew Dadang because one of his boys had been circumcised the day I visited his village. Also in the group that day was Ayung, a young man with a lot of talent who already had a little skill with a sewing machine. Ayung had been out of work for a long time. Then there was Indah, a leader in the village. He was older and more reserved, a man of few words. Each face in the group was familiar to me.

A few minutes into our conversation, one of the men reached for a bag I hadn't noticed. To my surprise he began to unfold a replica of one of the North Carolina quilts—made with the fabric that Dewi had bought at the market with the money I'd given her! I examined their work with amazement. Considering this was their first attempt at quilting, with absolutely no training—it was wonderful! I couldn't conceal my astonishment and delight.

These men were serious about this. Their fields and gardens weren't bringing in sufficient money to provide an education for their kids or meet their basic health needs. They had taken the initiative to make the pattern and figure out how to stitch the quilt together, even though a craft like this was not found in Nusandia at the time. They quickly worked as a team to get it done, and they enjoyed the whole process and figured it out on their own. They were motivated to learn more.

Dewi's colors were not what I would have chosen, but color preference is a cultural thing. At this point, the important issue was not the color but the quality of the work. Their stitching was reasonably good, and I was convinced that, with a little more help, they could become masters of the trade.

Dadang, the roadside soup seller

I knew it was worth investing some time to help Dewi and her relatives develop their sewing and quilting skills. As I praised the men for their diligence, they beamed with pride and satisfaction. They had travelled all day, at their own expense, to hear my verdict, and my positive response pleased them.

While the men relaxed in our living room and drank their tea, I went into our baby room and found a little patchwork quilt that my mom had sent me. It was a store-bought baby quilt, but the colors were great. I gave it to the men and suggested they try to duplicate it. As they left, I promised to try to find a buyer for the first quilt they had made.

It wasn't long before Dewi's friends and relatives completed their second quilt, then a third one. I could hardly keep up with them. The baby quilt they made was delightful and almost as nice as the original. I was amazed by their skill and ingenuity figuring out the patterns. Before long, they were pumping out baby quilts one after the other. Nusandians love to wrap their babies in blankets, even if it's warm.

Villagers make one of their first quilts.

It is one thing to make a quilt and quite another thing to sell it—especially if the colors aren't so good or the quality is questionable. Nevertheless, I took a few of the first quilts to some stores in the city, not knowing what to expect. Some of the Chinese shop owners (Most shops are owned by Chinese entrepreneurs.) agreed to place them in their windows on consignment. I explained the background behind the project and expressed my appreciation for their help.

Some of those quilts were quite crazy looking. I let everyone do what they wanted to do as far as colors because they were just learning, and they were using a lot of scrap material. They kept copying that original quilt in different colors. One quilt they brought me was so wild that I was convinced no one would want to buy it. I hid it on a shelf in the back of our storage room.

One day my new teammate Rhonda arrived in Nusandia with her husband, Spencer, and two small children. Rhonda was anxious to set up her home. They had not brought anything with them from the U.S. except their clothes.

"Do you know where I can buy some bedcovers?" Rhonda asked, checking her long list. "I want some blankets that are bright and cheerful." I wondered to myself what her definition of "cheerful" might be.

"The group I'm working with has a few quilts for sale," I responded. "They're starting to sell quite quickly, so we only have a handful of them. I'm not sure you'll like them." But Rhonda insisted on seeing what I had.

I showed Rhonda the quilts that were stacked in the corner of our living room. She immediately showed a genuine interest. "Wait, I have one more back in my pantry," I said as I darted for the kitchen. "It is really wild with clashing bright colors."

When she saw it, Rhonda loved it. With a big Texan laugh, she asked if she could take it home. The Lord had sent Rhonda to Nusandia to buy this crazy quilt! When I saw it on her bed I got a really good chuckle. Rhonda was fun and funky, and the quilt fit her personality. Beauty is definitely in the eye of the beholder, and she appreciated beauty that I had not seen in this quilt.

And then it started to happen—the quilts began to sell like hotcakes. Dewi and I allocated the proceeds so that they would cover the cost of materials and the labor of each person involved. Each time, I would save a little to invest in more cloth for the expanding project. Dewi helped me with the calculations. She helped establish fair compensation levels for all the workers, and we had a small notebook to record expenses and income.

Before long we could hardly keep up with the demand. We went into the city with some of our savings and purchased a treadle sewing machine. It looked like something that my great grandmother would have used a century ago. These were black machines with gold trim, made in China. They cost about $100 each, and they were simple, strong and easy to repair. They didn't require electricity. If we ever wanted electrical power on the machine, we could install a small power unit for $30 or $40. Dewi and I felt good about the purchases we were making.

Dewi was good at keeping the books.

Part of the fun and challenge involved training Dewi in her color choices. Because our customer base was largely wealthy Nusandians with Westernized tastes, or foreigners passing through Denalia, color combinations were important. We spent hours and hours together walking through crowded downtown bazaars, looking for the right textures and colors of cloth.

Before long, many of the shop owners knew me by name. Because no one could pronounce the "arl" in Arlene, they called me Lina (Lena). I was good at bargaining for the lowest price, and the shop owners soon realized I was no pushover. All it took was a few sentences in the Kantoli language, and they knew I'd been in the country a long time. I spoke the local language as well as the national language. Immediately, I'd get the same prices anyone else got. I was one of them.

Shopping in those alleys was actually a bit dangerous. It was very crowded, and people pressed in from every side. Of course, there was no fire marshal and no regulations to enforce. Once, a fire broke out in the very alley where Dewi and I did most of our shopping. When someone shouted, "Fire!", there was a huge stampede as people clamored to get out. Some died in the fire and others were trampled.

After each shopping expedition, Dewi and I would return home with huge bags of cloth. We recorded what we had spent that day and checked our budget, making sure we had plenty left over for wages.

The men of Banteng came back frequently with more and more quilts. I knew they were spending a lot of time and money travelling back and forth to the city and wondered if there was a more efficient way. Steve and I talked it over. We decided that for a season we would transform our home into a production center. Only bedrooms would be off limits. Dewi's relatives could stay and work for a whole week at a time, then return to their village for a week or for a weekend.

Behind our rented house was an old room for storage. Steve and some of the men cleared it out and painted it. It was small but sufficient for our needs. In it we placed the first two sewing machines that we purchased. A couple of the men had some experience with sewing machines, so they got the assignment. Others cut out cloth using patterns. Our living room was the cutting, arranging and hand stitching area. The men had their meals together, and some of them slept in our home. Others slept in Dewi's little house and the homes of other contacts they had in the city.

Meanwhile, Dewi and I designed new quilts, organized our ideas, shopped for fabric and supplies and kept track of the finances. We were on a roll, and nothing could stop the momentum. It was too late to turn back! The skills were "out of the bag," and news of what was going on in my home started to spread by word of mouth.

The project was getting fun and exciting. It was a real relationship-building time as we all worked together. There was a lot of laughter around the home with a festive community atmosphere, kind of like an Amish barn raising. Dewi cooked a huge pot of rice, fish and vegetables each day, and sometimes, as a special treat, we ate chicken.

Dadang, the gentle, soft-spoken man who until recently sold soup on the side of the road, had never used a sewing machine in his life, and he was one of the first to learn to work on the machines we bought. First I taught him how to sew squares together so they matched up. I taught him how to make small items like potholders and hot pads, and he soon graduated to larger squares and larger projects. When I told him he could make a large quilt, he was so proud of himself and eager to get started on his own big quilt. He carefully picked out hot pink and aqua blue cloth and asked if he could stay up late in the shed behind our home and just keep practicing his squares. Steve and I said, "No problem," and went to bed.

The next morning when the other quilters arrived, Dadang proudly displayed his handiwork. It was absolutely enormous! In fact, it was the size of two king-sized quilts combined. No one could believe the amount of work involved or that he had completed it overnight.

"You taught me how to put the squares together, so I just kept sewing," Dadang told me. "But you didn't teach me how to stop."

All the quilters burst out in laughter. They lovingly called it the "village quilt," saying that an entire village would be able to sleep under it. I gave it to Dadang because it was too unique and too large to sell. He loved it and took it home with him.

Dadang works on his "village quilt" in the back of our home.

Some friends in the U.S. who heard about what was going on in Nusandia sent me quilting magazines, and as I studied them I saw pictures of quilting tables—empty frames on which a large unfinished quilt can be clamped so that it's easier to do the hand stitching. This made total sense. Why hadn't I thought of it? Why hold the quilt or spread it out on the floor when it could be stretched over a rack?

We decided to design a quilt rack and call a carpenter in on the project. I thought of an older man who had made a little white table for Joy and Sarah and furniture for our porch.

Surely he could figure out how to make a quilting table, even though it would seem strange to him initially. I sent for Mr. Oman, and when he arrived, I showed him a picture of a quilting table and gave him some money to buy wood. Within a few days, we had a quilting table in our home and several women around it. Quickly they learned to sew the top of the quilt to the bottom of the quilt with the batting in between. Some of these women had never held needles before. Each woman would pin a little piece of her uniquely colored cloth onto the area that she was quilting. Each person would be paid based on how many sections they completed.

Dewi kept track of the wages and finances. We were careful to lock up the money at the end of the day. I took Dewi with me to the bank. It was the first time in her life that she had been in a bank. We opened an account. It wasn't that much money, but over time it started to add up.

The conversations around the quilting table and over the sewing machines energized me. My new friends, who were mostly Muslims from Dewi's village, felt free to ask me questions about life and faith. In fact, they loved talking about spiritual things. Unlike most Westerners, that's the world they live in. One of the questions they had was about the Holy Spirit. They had heard that Christians believed in three gods. I explained that we don't believe in three gods at all, but in one triune God. I loved these conversations, and I went through whatever door the Lord opened.

Our business kept growing, and soon others began to hear about the opportunities for work at the little home down a crowded street in Denalia. In a city of two million with an unemployment rate of 25 percent, you can imagine how the word spread. The women also began to show up at my home.

Since their husbands or relatives were quilting in my home, they felt secure enough to join in on the project.

Steve and I began making Sunday visits to an isolated Christian village called Pangon. It was a long drive, close to an hour and a half each way, but we enjoyed worshipping with the small congregation of Kantoli believers. It was a Dutch Reformed congregation, and the services seemed rather ritualistic to us, yet we hoped to be an encouragement to them. I wondered what might happen if we worked with these people more closely and provided practical skills as well as theological training.

The women from Pangon were anxious to learn.

One day some Christian women from Pangon came to visit us. They looked around our home and were amazed to see so much activity. They had heard that we were providing work for a lot of people.

"How many people work here?" one of them ventured.

"I'm not sure. Quite a few—maybe twenty or thirty?" I could tell from their expressions that the wheels of their minds were turning.

127

"Did all these people already know how to sew?"

"No, we taught them. We're trying to help people who don't have skills but are willing to learn and work hard. Why?"

"Are these people Muslims?" The group's apparent spokeswoman lowered her voice, not wanting to be heard by the workers around us. She gazed into my eyes with heart-penetrating sincerity.

"Yes, they are." I wondered where she was going with her line of questioning.

"We need help, too. As you know, we're from a Christian village. There are very few of us in this part of the island. We've been forced to establish our own village in order to survive. We don't have many opportunities to work and find jobs because Muslims won't hire us. It's good that you are helping Muslims, but what about the people they persecute. Shouldn't they be helped, too?"

She was right. Weren't these dear ladies in equal, if not greater, financial need than the men and women working all around us? I explained to the Pangon ladies that I wanted to have a friendship ministry to Muslims in order to show them the love of Christ—yet I couldn't dispute their logic. Christians, too, must be blessed.

This encounter with the ladies of Pangon shifted the project to a new level. Steve and I decided, wherever possible, to employ Christians and Muslims side by side. Mixing the two would be a challenge, but it would also be a powerful spiritual experiment. In this society believers are normally sidelined, if not completely ostracized, by the Muslim majority. While there are mosques on every corner, churches are almost never permitted, at least in the rural areas. In the rare event that someone tried to construct a Christian house of worship, it would almost invariably be burned to the ground. After all, this was a Muslim province—not a place for followers of Jesus.

It would be fascinating to see the two worlds meet right here in our own home. Neither group would naturally gravitate toward working with the other, but when people are desperate for work, they will do almost anything, even if it means sitting next to an infidel at a quilting table. Furthermore, I was not forcing anyone into a church building. I was simply creating a comfortable, honest working environment in my home.

As Steve and I talked it over, a subtle but important shift was taking place in our thinking. Rather than building this effort around Muslims and with Muslim leadership, why not build it around Kantoli Christians—an "endangered species" in their own homeland? There were very few of them, but they were here, and they represented the future growth of the church among the Kantoli. Instead of Christians being persecuted by Muslims, we could try to create a place where Christians could be a blessing to Muslims by providing them with jobs. As the two groups worked side by side, barriers might crumble, and the truth of the gospel could be communicated more effectively. The day-to-day routine of working and eating together could become a fertile context for spiritual impact.

Before long, believers from Pangon and other areas started joining in. Steve and I were excited by all that was happening. After the initial novelty of Muslims meeting Kantoli Christians for the first time, everyone generally relaxed. Muslims realized Christians were real people with the same needs and hopes. God was clearly opening a wonderful door of opportunity—more than we ever dreamed when we set foot on this land years before. Our home was full of people excitedly cutting cloth, arranging the pieces on the floor, stitching them together and transporting the sheets and padding back to their villages where others could join in the laborious task of hand stitching.

One of the joys was to see these people talk with each other. The barriers between Muslims and Christians began to melt, and conversations flowed from the heart. I saw openness that I had not seen before in my Muslim friends. I saw Christians touched with compassion for their Muslim colleagues, rather than fear or resentment toward them.

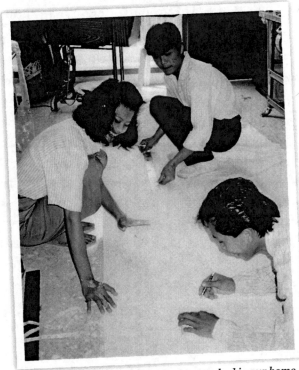

There was a lot of laughter as they worked in our home.

It would have been difficult for me as a foreigner to make frequent trips to Dewi's isolated village. It was many hours away, and I would have looked so out of place as a tall, light-skinned American woman. Even if I had been able to visit frequently, the village leaders would have eventually become suspicious about my presence and motives. The Muslim leaders from the local mosques would have begun warning the villagers to avoid me, or at least to disregard anything I might say, especially if it had to do with matters of faith. Knowing this, God had arranged something remarkable. *He had brought the village to me.* He had answered the prayer I had prayed on the mountainside of Dewi's village: "Lord, make me a blessing to these people."

Each day in my home, I would awaken just in time to welcome 15 or 20 people right in my own living room. One of the benefits of work in an Asian environment is that there are few, if any, restrictions on conducting business out of one's home. When people are hungry and half the population is unemployed or underemployed, no one bothers with such regulations and rules. Those sorts of restrictions are the domain of wealthier countries where people throw out their extra food and have the luxury of thinking up new ways to spend their money.

I didn't even need to walk down the street, much less navigate a variety of public transportation vehicles across our city of two million or over the mountains to their villages! Laughter and conversation filled our home. These new friends were thoroughly enjoying themselves in my living room, appreciating my food and hospitality, and perhaps most valuable of all learning how to make a living for themselves and their families. They were experiencing something they had never in their lives experienced before: genuine Christian love. And there were no loud voices or mosque loudspeakers warning them against associating with infidels or brainwashing them with messages of fear and hellfire.

Chapter 11

QUILT OF TEARS

- - - - - - - -

You keep track of all my sorrows. You have collected all my tears in your bottle. You have recorded each one in your book.

—Psalm 56:8 NLT

Turning our home into a beehive of activity gave us a sense of excitement and progress, but it also had its downsides. For one thing, we had a hard time keeping track of who was coming and who was going. Late one afternoon Steve and the girls and I prepared to leave on a short overnight trip. The house was quiet. I checked to see if all the quilters had gone home, and there didn't seem to be anyone around, so we loaded our bags into the car, locked the house and left. It wasn't until we returned the next evening that we discovered three of the young men had been working in the shed in our back yard—a place I'd missed in my last-minute pre-departure check. The three men recounted their humorous story after we returned. They'd left the work-room the previous afternoon to go home. To their surprise, they found the house totally locked up. Our house, like many in the city, had a fairly high wall around it, with barbed wire on top. The three men were unable to leave. Nightfall came, and they became very hungry. They climbed the fruit trees in the backyard looking for something to eat. Realizing the men were missing, Dewi and her concerned relatives came over to our home only to find it locked up. They yelled over the fence to see if the men were there. Sure enough, the men hollered back. They ended up sleeping under the stars with only a little fruit to eat.

Deki working in our garage

Our second house was situated at the end of a very narrow alley in a crowded hillside neighborhood. By this time, we had an inexpensive used vehicle. The corners were so tight, we could barely squeeze it into our driveway. We were aware that many people watched all of the quilters going in and out of our home. I always felt safe when there were a lot of people around.

The evenings were relatively quiet, however. We enjoyed having a little time to ourselves, exhausted as we often were, after a day's work.

�֎

One night we tucked Joy and Sarah into bed a little early. I headed toward bed as well. Steve was going to play tennis early in the morning, so he leaned his tennis racket against the wall next to our bed where he could reach it easily in the early morning darkness the next day. At about 2 a.m., I was awakened by the sound of a faint thud. Thinking one of the girls may have fallen out of bed in their room across from ours, I got out of bed to check on them. I slipped across into their room and checked their bunk bed. In the darkness I could see that both of them were fast asleep, like two little angels. A bit puzzled as to where the noise had come from, I turned and stepped back into the little hallway, heading toward our room. In the darkness I happened to glance to my right, toward the dining table and kitchen. To my shock, just a few feet away from me, I saw the silent, threatening shadow of a man with a crowbar raised in the air, as if preparing to strike me!

Instinctively I let out a startled cry. I didn't know what to do, so I just screamed, "Police, police!" Steve heard my yelling and slowly awoke from his sound sleep, trying to make sense of what was happening. He grabbed the first thing that he could find—his tennis racket—and came running out of our room toward me. I yelled and pointed, and Steve rushed past me toward our living room just in time to see four men disappear into the shadows around the corner of the wall. At first we thought we'd trapped them in the living room and that perhaps they were hiding behind our curtains. We weren't quite sure what to do. But the more we peered into the shadows and waited, the more we began to conclude they were not there! We noticed the curtains were blowing in the wind. This was unusual because there were no louvers in that window—no way for air to get through. It was just a big sheet of glass. As we got closer and pulled the curtains apart we realized the men had taken out the entire picture window, frame and all. We later found the sheet of glass lying unbroken on the ground in front of our house.

A few neighbors quickly materialized in the moonlight outside our front door, drawn by my initial screams. They just shook their heads. The burglars had been in the process of picking up our television in the living room (the television that Ardi had given us a few years earlier) when I had interrupted their work. Our neighbors assured me there was no point in reporting this event to the police, or calling for their help, because there was a good chance the police were complicit in the crime. Even the community night watchman, a fixture in virtually every Nusandian city neighborhood, had probably been paid off. How else could the men have gotten their little pick-up truck so near to our house at that time of the night?

When the quilters came in the morning there were a lot of discussions regarding the whole incident. The conclusion was that these kinds of incidents were unavoidable in this environment. In fact, our neighbor informed us that we were "lucky." He recounted how a thief came into his home one night while he and his family were asleep. The thief couldn't find much to steal, so he just took all the clothes from their closet! When our neighbors awoke in the morning they had no clothes to wear!

Our neighbors and the quilters told us stories about how gangs of thieves often perform black magic to put people into a sound sleep, so they don't wake up while their possessions are being stolen. Needless to say, it took me a while to sleep well the next several weeks. Even Steve had a hard time sleeping soundly for a couple of months. We kept wondering if the thieves would pay us a return visit to finish the work they'd begun. We reinforced our windows and added some bars, but we knew there wasn't much that we could do but commit ourselves once again into God's care.

One weekend I went on a ladies retreat while Steve watched Joy and Sarah. In his typical way, he assured me that all would go well. While I was gone, Steve and the girls went to a big Kantoli wedding. After returning home that night, Steve did not feel well. Perhaps he'd eaten some food that had been out in the hot air too long. He put the girls to bed and then went to bed himself. In the middle of the night, he woke up feeling really sick and vomited quite violently. Then he felt a lot better and went back to bed.

The next morning, Steve felt better, but something was different. He felt like he wasn't able to take a deep breath. Disregarding it, he went about his usual busy schedule.

When I returned home from the retreat, Steve mentioned that he was feeling a bit strange and short of breath. He has a high tolerance for pain, or maybe it was just his high drive that kept him pursuing his normal routine of work around town for a couple of days. Finally he decided he should mention his shortness of breath to an American doctor who was studying language in our city.

The doctor told Steve over the phone to go get an x-ray first and then to meet him in front of the grocery store that evening. Steve rode his motorcycle to the nearest hospital and had an x-ray taken. Steve asked the technician what he thought of the x-ray. "Looks fine to me," said the technician. "There is nothing wrong. Your lungs look perfect."

Later that night, Steve met the American doctor in a grocery store parking lot. The doctor held up the x-ray to a streetlight and studied it for a moment. Then he turned to Steve and said,

"Where are you headed next?" Steve replied, "I have a meeting on the east side of town."

"Not anymore," the doctor said. "You're going straight to the hospital. This is serious."

"Why, what's the problem?"

"Your left lung has completely collapsed. If the second one goes, you're a dead man."

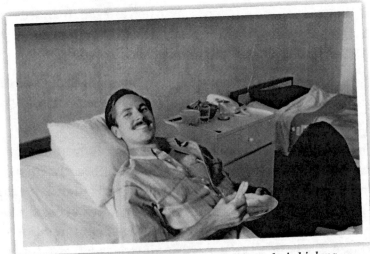

Steve enjoys a meal after the doctor put a tube in his lung.

With that Steve decided it was probably wise to cancel his plans and ride his motorcycle straight to the hospital. He had to visit a couple of hospitals before he found one that had a lung specialist on duty. A half hour later the Nusandian doctor confirmed the diagnosis of the American doctor. Steve would need surgery to insert a tube into his left lung cavity so that the lung could re-inflate over time.

"When do you want your surgery?" the Nusandian doctor asked Steve as he sat on the bench in his little office.

"We might as well do it now," Steve replied. "I've already cancelled my evening plans."

"Okay, let's get you into the surgical room and do it now," the doctor replied nonchalantly.

On his way to the surgical room, Steve located a hospital phone and gave me a call to let me know that his lung had collapsed, and he was going into surgery.

"Right now?" I asked.

"Yep, right now."

Steve was never one to waste time.

Before I could even get to the hospital, the doctor cut a hole in Steve's chest and inserted a tube. Shortly before the knife went in, Steve brushed a huge cockroach off the side table next to his bed. Everything seemed a bit surreal, but somehow nothing much fazed us anymore. The unexpected was no longer unexpected.

✂

The workers' openness to spiritual things impressed me. At the same time we were experiencing a lot of strange things. I was aware of the Kantoli fear of evil spirits, but one day it came home to me more than usual. As Steve and the girls and I were sitting down to eat dinner, I noticed a small, flat object on the wall above the kitchen door. I went over to see what it was. A piece of paper with Arabic writing on it had been folded over many times and then nailed to the wall. It had been covered in plastic and painted over by someone.

This was our second home in Denalia. Unlike our first home, which we'd rented from Christians, a Muslim family owned this home. On a hunch, Steve and I went to each door post and window in the house and found that each door and window had a similar paper over it. Steve took a small hammer and pried each amulet off the wall. The next day Dewi confirmed that these were Islamic amulets that were meant to ward off evil spirits. Kantoli people would typically pay the local Imam to write verses from the Quran on little pieces of paper and place them strategically in places where evil spirits were likely to pass. Lowering her voice, Dewi added that many houses and buildings are dedicated with the sacrifice of a goat or chicken. Its body is buried under or near the building in order to ward off evil. The idea of appeasing evil spirits is common in their culture. It wasn't entirely unusual, in fact, for parents to "make a deal with the devil" by dedicating one of their children to him.

Me with Nusandian school girls

Steve called some of the quilters together in the back yard. He explained the power of God through Christ over the demonic realm. He read a couple of Bible verses and told them that, as followers of Christ, he and I had no reason to be afraid of evil spirits. Then he lit a match and burned the amulets. It was a rather graphic demonstration to the workers of the many important differences in our worldviews.

It was during these weeks of excitement and activity in early 1992 that we encountered one of our first major setbacks. Although I absolutely loved the local food, when lunch was served, I suddenly had to look the other way. I couldn't bear the smell of the food frying—even my favorite Nusandian dish of spicy spinach, chili peppers and rice. Steve looked at my eyes and told me to look in the mirror. I was shocked at what I saw. My eyes were quite yellow, which could mean only one thing: I had hepatitis.

God knew I was worn out and needed the rest, and that is exactly what the doctor prescribed—a month or more of rest. But how was I going to help the quilters get their projects done? Our business was really taking off because several ladies in the city had recently placed orders with us. It was a dream come true to have orders because that meant we already had buyers for what we were working on. The workers knew they could continue to work and eat.

If ever there was a time to get hepatitis, this was not it. I rationalized that surely the doctor didn't mean I had to go on total bed rest, did he? Maybe now and then I could sneak out of bed and spend time with the quilters going over their projects. But I couldn't do even that. My skin rapidly turned yellow, and I lost all my energy. Each day I lay in bed wishing I could participate but finding myself unable to do so. At best, I would advise and encourage Dewi from my bed, offering suggestions on color choices and inspecting their work as she would bring items to me.

Hepatitis is a liver disease that brings on serious fatigue and nausea. I couldn't eat anything that was fried, and in Nusandia almost all the food is fried. Whenever a meal was cooked in our home, it would make me feel nauseated. Even worse, I began to itch terribly. At nightfall, with little else on my mind, I would be horribly uncomfortable. I coated my skin with anti-itch cream, but it didn't seem to help. Sometimes I would scratch so hard I would bleed. My legs had big red streaks down them from the scratching.

Dewi, my best friend, knew how uncomfortable I was. During the midnight hours, she took it upon herself to help me get my mind off the itching. She also made it possible for Steve to get a decent night's rest. Because I was sick, Steve was carrying an extra heavy load, caring for the two girls and me while still maintaining his many teaching and leadership responsibilities. I was so grateful to Dewi for her companionship. During the quiet night hours, we talked about everything under the sun. As everyone else slept, God was doing a deep spiritual work in our lives. I was getting to know this intelligent woman much more intimately, and she was sharing stories about her life and asking significant questions about mine. These conversations would not have been possible if others had been listening.

Night after night I would lie on the sofa while Dewi would stitch a quilt or rub my legs. She was always doing something constructive. The quilt she was working on was one we had designed together. We had carefully coordinated the colors in light blues. We knew it would be a masterpiece and would sell quickly. Dewi had fashioned a circular wooden hoop, and her small hands moved swiftly as we talked, adding stitch to stitch. She was amazingly accurate and consistent.

First we talked about the events of the day—who said what, what had been accomplished, what problems had been encountered. Often we'd share some uncontrolled laughter about something silly that had happened. Then we would talk about the business aspects of the project and dream of what this might become in the future. How could we get more capital for expansion? Could we rent another house specifically for this project, so this beehive of activity could be separated from our family life?

Sometimes we talked about the animals back in her village that she had invested in and how they were breeding and selling. Dewi was a businesswoman at heart. She had natural instincts in this area and knew how every penny had been spent. She also had her extended family and village at heart. She wanted to feed them and see them prosper. Her generosity was inspiring to me.

Dewi stitched as we talked.

Inevitably, sometime during the night, the conversation would drift into matters of the heart. Sometimes we talked about difficult experiences of the past. Often we cried softly together in the semi-darkness. As Dewi began to open up and share her life experiences, I gained a deeper understanding of her world. She and her people were friendly and hospitable.

They loved their land—the fertile mountain slopes and bubbling natural springs that nourished their fields. Their language was exquisite, a matter of great pride. They competed with each other to see who could invent the best tongue twisters or word plays. They were incredibly musical and artistic.

Beneath it all, however, not far past the smiles and laughter, these people were hurting deeply. On one occasion she told me of an experience she'd had years earlier. As a young village girl desperate for work, she'd agreed to move to the big city to take a job from a distant aunt and uncle. They agreed to let her sleep on the floor of a small room in their home. One night her uncle slipped into her room and raped her. This happened more than once and had a devastating effect on her.

I was shocked to learn that this was a relatively common experience. Often when a young woman was given a job, she was expected to provide sexual favors in return. This kind of behavior was tolerated as part of the "dark side" of their culture.

"But, Lina, why are you so surprised?" Dewi said when she saw my horrified reaction. "This is my destiny. Muslims believe that because Allah has all power, anything that happens must be part of his will. There is nothing I can do to change it. Who am I to fight against Allah?"

I sat there motionless, pondering how to respond.

"Dewi, the God of the Bible came to earth to heal those wounds and to free you. He loves you and wants you to be free and to know him as a friend."

"But God cannot be known personally," Dewi said. "He is too distant. He doesn't care about me individually."

"God does want to know you personally, Dewi. That's the amazing thing—we can know Him."

144

Traumatized by the abuse she had experienced, Dewi eventually fled her uncle's home and found her way back to her village. She felt defiled and alone. A betrayal of this sort brings scars beyond words. As she shared, tears of pain fell on to the beautiful quilt Dewi was stitching. Dewi shared story after story. I was amazed at how anyone could endure such things. I longed for the healing finger of God to reach down out of heaven and touch her hurting soul.

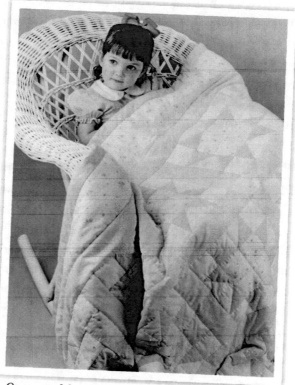

Our second daughter Sarah with Dewi's "quilt of tears"

Night after night I listened to Dewi and watched the quilt in her hands take shape. In time it was a beautiful masterpiece. I began to think of it as a quilt of tears. In my mind I associated this particular quilt with the painful and emotional stories Dewi was telling me. I was a foreigner from a different place, yet she was entrusting me with her secrets—the scars and bruises of life in a broken world. My own difficulties and inconveniences faded into insignificance. Yes, I had hepatitis, but God had blessed me and was at that very moment continuing to bless me in innumerable ways. He'd given me a marvelous family, the best mother and father imaginable and a graduate degree from a wonderful school. I was privileged to be born in the United States. I had grown up knowing that God loved me with an eternal love and that He had expressed this love on a cross 2,000 years ago. I had a wonderful husband who honored and cherished me and loved sharing life's journey with me. We had two gorgeous little girls. We had food on our table—enough to share with others. Precious friends back home loved us and prayed for us.

Dewi's beautiful quilt of tears was eventually sold. It was hard emotionally for me to see it go, but it had to sell to help us carry on the work. Its new owner had no idea what it represented to me—a reminder of a friend's personal pain and the first glimmers of future hope in her life. Those inexpensive pieces of cloth, stitched together into something unique and precious, represented a person's life to me. She was not just any person, but a close friend whom I had come to know and love, someone who knew what it was like to really suffer. How had Dewi survive? How did anyone survive without the tender and compassionate presence of a loving God?

It was during one of these midnight talks that I put a video into our VHS player. It was a video recently produced in the heart language of the Kantoli people, one of the projects that our team and some local Christians had worked on together a year or two earlier. It was called the *Jesus* film and was a simple re-enactment of the life of Christ, taken word for word from the Gospel of Luke. It had been translated into hundreds of languages around the world and was now finally available in the heart language of 35 million Kantoli people. The recorded voices of Jesus and His disciples and other personalities were familiar to us. They were the voices of some of the Kantoli Christian friends with whom Steve worked.

As Dewi and I watched, my own heart was moved. I felt like I was witnessing the life and teachings of Jesus not through familiar Western eyes, but from the perspective of a Kantoli Muslim. From time to time, I glanced at Dewi's face in the shadows next to me to get a feel for how she was responding. She was obviously riveted by the story, laughing as Jesus welcomed the little children onto His lap and captivated as Jesus cast out demons, healed the lame, opened blind eyes and raised the dead. Here was a man who spoke the truth, loved justice and honored the women in His life. He spoke out against authoritarian leaders who lived hypocritical lives and exploited the poor. He didn't hesitate to throw the cheaters and extortionists out of God's holy temple.

Dewi was especially amazed at the interactions Jesus had with women. He related to them with obvious respect and tenderness. Rather than exploit them, He affirmed them and cared deeply about their needs. When Christ was beaten mercilessly, then forced to carry His cross out of the city onto a rocky hill, big tears rolled down Dewi's cheeks. Jesus' mother and the other women who loved Him and had long attended to His needs followed at a distance, mourning. It seemed to be the women who loved and appreciated Him the most. Dewi knew what it was like to be beaten and used by a man. She'd never known a man like this.

I explained to Dewi that Jesus suffered voluntarily. As the soldiers drove the iron pegs through His hands, Jesus was thinking of Dewi and her family and the people of her village. Through her tears I could sense that Dewi had taken a few more steps on a long spiritual journey. Questions and longings flooded her mind. I knew better than to rush the process. The Spirit of God, the master quilter, was doing His delicate work on the threads of Dewi's life.

The late-night talks went on for weeks. I was concerned that Dewi got so little sleep. It was understandable that I was unable to sleep because of my hepatitis, but for Dewi this was not healthy. I wondered how she could have the physical stamina to carry on with the chores of the day. And, unlike some, she never took naps.

When I protested about Dewi's late nights and suggested that she get more rest, she opened up to me about another part of her life. She said that she hadn't had a good night's rest since childhood. When she was a little girl, she was given two demonic spirits to be her life-long companions. This was a common practice among the Kantoli.

Dewi found herself caught in an endless web of fear and deceit. These demons never left her alone. They talked with her while she worked in her garden. When she would fall asleep at night, the demons would awaken her and harass her. They had distinct voices, personalities and names. To her, this was an accepted, though painful, reality. She longed to be free from demonic powers that did nothing but tease and intimidate her. She found some small comfort in knowing that she was not alone. Many, if not most, of her friends had similar demonic companions who regularly controlled or interfered with their lives.

In addition to the scars of sexual exploitation, I saw that demonic abuse was an equal or even greater factor in Dewi's life. For the Kantoli, life was inextricably intertwined with the spirit world. Though they were Muslims, every significant aspect of life—the planting of crops, harvest ceremonies, the conception and rearing of children, marriages and funerals— all of these had strong connections in the spirit world. Nothing of significance is done without placating or seeking the blessings of the demonic powers that ruled their land.

I put my arm around Dewi's shoulders, and we sat quietly together in the dim light. All was quiet except for the crickets outside. Sensing the Spirit's nudging, I began to pray audibly and earnestly for Dewi. I prayed against the supernatural forces that were conspiring against her mind and body. I pleaded in the authority of the Lord Jesus Christ for Dewi's spiritual emancipation. Dewi welcomed my prayers. She embraced me with deep appreciation. Though she came from a profoundly different religious context, she sensed that I understood what she was experiencing and was not discounting or judging her for it. She also felt that my prayers had real power. The battle for spiritual freedom in Dewi's life was well underway. I sensed hope from God ... and resistance from a very real enemy.

Chapter 12

DOCTOR'S ORDERS

Don't get tired of doing what is good.
Don't get discouraged and give up, for we will reap a harvest
of blessing at the appropriate time.

—GALATIANS 6:9 NLT

I was very anxious to get back to our quilting enterprise, but the doctor's orders kept me in bed. The business kept growing—which was wonderful—yet at the same time we knew that things couldn't continue as they were. We were adding more and more workers, and by now, our home was overrun with quilters. I didn't want them to go, but we were running out of space and needed some privacy. It seemed as if an entire village had moved into our home. If sustained indefinitely, this level of activity would begin affecting our family life—and it would also stifle the growth of this movement. We needed to find ways to release and diversify this vision for greater growth. We prayed about it and asked God for wisdom.

Around this time my mother paid us a visit. She was used to international travel and couldn't wait to see her granddaughters. Dad and Mom's work with Pioneers had expanded rapidly over the years. The organization now had workers in more than 40 countries. God had richly rewarded Dad and Mom's step of faith when they left the business world to use their gifts in world missions.

My mother Peggy with Kantoli quilters

Mom got right into our quilting enterprise. The quilters loved her because she was kind and had grey hair. This made her wise and worthy of respect. Older people are honored in Asia. She used hand motions to communicate the best she could or spoke English loudly and slowly, thinking that might help the workers understand her better. Mom laughed at the different personalities of the people and helped me with colors and new quilt ideas. She too was sensing that, although the activity within the home was exciting, it was also exhausting, and I needed to pace myself. Shortly before she returned to the U.S., she decided that, instead of buying souvenirs to take home, she would give me the money to purchase another sewing machine.

She knew the eternal significance of what God was doing, and adding another machine—and thus another quilter—brought joy to her heart.

But that wasn't all. When Mom went home, she began telling others about the amazing things that were happening through this self-help program. One of the people she talked to was her friend Linda Ryan. Linda had a heart for the poor, having started a ministry for special-needs children. To our great encouragement, one day when I was sick, I received a check in the mail from Linda for $3,000! She said she was sending it specifically so that we could rent a separate house for the quilting project.

I was so grateful for the gift, and so was Steve! He went out right away and found a large house just two blocks away. With $3,000 he was able to sign a three-year contract. What a provision! I was so excited. Steve, Dewi and the quilters wasted no time moving all the equipment and supplies out of our house and to the new location.

I could hardly wait to see the new operation, but the doctor's orders were clear: I still wasn't completely well, and he wanted me to rest. The first few weeks, I was a good girl and stayed in bed, but then I couldn't stand it any longer. I missed the quilters. I had to take care of some needs over at the rented house, so I walked a couple of blocks and spent a few hours going over things with the workers. It was fun to be with them again, and I realized how much I enjoyed all the people and the hurricane of progress. We had some laughter together and some tea, and I walked home somewhat reassured that they had everything under control.

With the move to the new home, we decided it was time to come up with a name for the business: HeartCraft. It seemed an apt description for a project that was touching so many lives and hearts in practical ways. We were excited to have more space. In fact we even had an upstairs room, above the main quilting center, that also doubled as a couple of guest rooms. Steve and I had more visitors than we knew what to do with! Thankfully we were able to put some of our visitors over in the guestrooms right over the HeartCraft quilters. This way the guests could also get a good dose of the culture, language and food of the people.

Some of the quilters had never interacted with a foreigner before, so this was a new experience for all. Dewi went out of her way to serve them by bringing them a bucket of hot water for their showers each morning. One visitor, Mr. Anthony, was a rather portly man who came on a team with a pastor for the purpose of leading worship times. He was an excellent pianist and singer. What we did not realize was that he also had a toupee, which he kept on his head when he was out in public and removed when he was alone in his room.

One morning Dewi and a couple of the ladies went up the stairs to deliver the hot water. When they went into his room, Mr. Anthony looked normal. They greeted him, put down the bucket of steaming water and quickly left the room. Suddenly Dewi realized she had forgotten something upstairs and went back up, only to find that Mr. Anthony now had no hair on his head. In her shock she let out a little shriek of surprise, much to Mr. Anthony's embarrassment. Dewi later said to me. "I had no idea that American men can take their hair on and off whenever they want to." For days, this event was a main topic of conversation among the quilters. Mr. Anthony never knew just how famous he became among the quilters of Nusandia.

Because I was in bed with hepatitis and wasn't there to make day-to-day decisions, the workers had more freedom to make them. They were delighted to take matters into their own hands. I was learning that running a business in an Asian country is completely different from doing it in the U.S. For example, the Kantoli people are so polite that sometimes I couldn't tell what they were really thinking or feeling. For one thing, they never wanted to give me bad news or admit they didn't know how to do something. Sometimes they would rather ruin a huge quilt by doing it wrong than ask me for help. They might get embarrassed, or *ulam* as they called it. *Ulam* involves loss of face, and the desire to avoid feeling *ulam* is a powerful motivator in this culture. It's difficult for a Westerner to understand, but for a Kantoli, it's the worst thing that can happen.

In a business setting in my home culture, I could be direct and just say what was needed, but in this culture the worst thing for me to do was be direct. I had to be very careful not to offend these dear people by sharing correction or suggestions too directly. Sometimes it would take an hour or so to explain what needed to be done. Instead of saying, even in a nice tone of voice, "You did this wrong," I had to say, "Maybe we can try a different way." For me it was like walking on eggshells as I tried not to offend people.

You can imagine how I reacted (or wanted to react) when I couldn't go to the store to buy more fabric. The workers realized they were running low on cloth, and they headed downtown to buy more. They were specifically looking for something that would complement our remaining cloth. Dewi was all for the excursion. She had been shopping with me many times and knew what looked good and what didn't. She also figured she would spare me the pressure of thinking that I had to choose all the materials when she could now do it herself.

I knew she wanted to show me she was able to lead in my absence. I had no other option because I was sick in bed, and Dewi's reasoning sounded good—until the workers came home and showed me what they bought. The fabric was bright green with little purple fish splashed all over it. The complementary fabric was bright orange with blue fish. Not only were the colors absolutely garish, but the cloth itself was not at all the quality that we needed.

When I saw it, I almost fainted. And they didn't buy just a few meters, either. They had a huge roll! Our hard-earned money had been spent on fish fabric. In Nusandia you can't return purchased items like you can in the U.S. I felt sick inside.

As carefully as I could, trying not to show my disappointment, I asked, "Why did you buy this fabric?"

"It was on sale."

"But, what do you think we should do with it?"

"Make quilts, of course! Don't you like fish?"

"Not everyone likes fish, and it will take a long time to use these huge rolls of fabric" I explained, trying to appear calm and collected.

No one seemed concerned. All I got were blank stares. Then Ayung spoke up with a smile, "People here love fish. We eat fish from our ponds all the time! Look, they are even in bright and cheerful colors."

I could tell I wasn't getting anywhere. We were on a limited budget. How would we sell hundreds of fish quilts? I dreaded the thought of trying to market them.

"Well, it's going to be a miracle if any of the fish quilts sell," I replied.

To accelerate the usage of the fabric we began to put it in all kinds of products—from potholders to purses. Virtually every item had fish in it. I even had dreams about fish.

It turned out that they were right. Someone whose sons loved fishing would buy a few quilts. Another person who loved to eat fish would grab one. Still others who simply liked fish would buy a quilt. Was I the only one who had a problem with the purple fish quilts? I guess I was. It took a year, but every single one of the fish quilts eventually sold. I learned that if God could multiply the fish and bread to feed 5,000 people, then He could certainly make fish quilts sell. He is a God of miracles, and He demonstrated it to me right in front of the quilters. This was a strong reminder that ultimately this project belonged to God, and He was able to take care of it. My job was to be faithful. The Lord also wanted me to have a few laughs along the way.

All the mistakes were not so easily rectified, however. While I was still sick in bed, a woman from New Zealand came to the quilters with two big bags of cloth. She had always wanted to make a quilt for her daughter who was now getting married, but she never had the time. Then she heard of HeartCraft. One of the bags she brought us contained a priceless treasure of memories from her daughter's life—delicate baby clothes, tiny dresses with adorable prints, youthful skirts and blouses. These were all items that her daughter had worn when she was small, and the proud mother wanted us to make them into a beautiful quilt that she could present to her daughter as a wedding gift.

It was a wonderful idea! The only problem was that our workers were not yet skilled enough to do what this lady was requesting. Yet, being Kantoli, they couldn't lose face by saying, "No." So they said, "Yes." I was too sick to help them figure it out so I just let them make their own decisions.

They enthusiastically accepted the bag with the precious baby clothes in it and nodded politely as if to say they understood the mother's instructions. She was delighted.

The woman from New Zealand also gave the workers a second bag of scrap cloth unrelated to the first one. It was worthless cloth that she just wanted to donate to the quilters who were in training, to help them practice their new skills. They

157

were ugly scraps of cloths—some of the cloth even had red elephants on it—but it was perfect for training new workers. The staff thanked her and assured her that they would use it. The lady left with a smile of satisfaction on her face.

Dewi was a reasonably good leader, but by this time she had too much to do. She was learning what it was like to lead in my absence and to juggle finances, sales, wages, special orders, and regular production—not to mention overseeing the cooks who made lunches for everyone and the team that washed the quilts that had stains.

You can guess what happened. Somehow the two bags got mixed—not only mixed up but mixed together. The sweet little adorable dresses were cut up and mixed with the ugly scraps from the donated bag. The result was a beautifully stitched wedding-ring quilt using a horrible mixture of fabrics. Who in the world would want to give or receive a wedding-ring quilt with red elephants on it? It was embarrassing. I was too sick to cry and too weak to yell. Why couldn't the workers instinctively know that a red elephant should not appear in a wedding-ring quilt? Why could they not recognize that soft delicate colors should not mix with loud bright colors? Had I not taught them anything?

To make matters worse, some of the little girl prints were starting to appear in the beginner's potholders. And some of the bright scraps were appearing in other large quilts. It was a mess, and there was no way to retrieve the proper cloth and start over. This is a nightmare, I thought.

I wondered what I might do to apologize to this sweet woman from New Zealand. I agonized over the reaction that she might have. I felt that saying it was a mistake was not enough. We were making too many mistakes. This one hurt. It was sentimental cloth that she had collected and saved for years, and we had totally botched the project. When the lady came back for her quilt, she was shocked. The expression on her face was like something out of a movie, but she composed herself and was surprisingly forgiving. I ended up giving her the horrible, well-made wedding quilt with the wrong colors. Maybe she would have a good laugh about it one day; maybe not. I also let her have any other quilt she wanted for free. In the end she was all right, and I don't think we lost a customer.

To avoid repeating these kinds of mistakes, Dewi and I started to tape big notes on every special order. We were putting a lot of time and money into each quilt, so I felt it was worth the effort to ensure a quality outcome. We even made pictures of what the finished quilt should look like. We talked about each special order and made things as clear as humanly possible. Still, it was not easy to communicate every detail. Sometimes I wondered, *Were the people listening to me or were they, frankly, just stubborn?* Often, when I wanted a piece of cloth cut vertically with the design, they would cut it horizontally. It was funny at times, but then it got really frustrating. If I softly corrected someone about their quality, then I might not see them for days because they were *malu*. It was a constant challenge to improve the quality without losing my quilters, who had become my friends as well.

After I'd had hepatitis for a few weeks, I made a trip to the doctor's office hoping for a good report. The doctor took a blood test and asked if I was behaving myself.

"Absolutely!" I replied. "I feel much better." I was hoping he would let me resume normal activities.

"Not so!" he said. "I saw you! You were not being good and staying in bed. In fact, the other day when I was on my way to work, I saw you walking down the road."

He caught me! Not only did the doctor scold me for disobeying his orders, but he ordered me to have even more rest.

Didn't he know I had things to do? Quilting can't just stop! I wondered if I should give him a free fish quilt to pacify him. Maybe a bribe would work? The doctor said it would take time to heal. Patience is not my greatest quality, but he insisted that I discipline myself and rest a few more weeks. I chuckled as I remembered a sign I'd seen somewhere: "Women who behave themselves rarely make history."

Chapter 13

A MODERN-DAY BOAZ

- - - - - - - -

When you are harvesting your crops and forget to bring in a
bundle of grain from your field, don't go back to get it.
Leave it for the foreigners, orphans, and widows. Then the Lord
your God will bless you in all you do.

—DEUTERONOMY 24:19 NLT

As I slowly began to feel better, I knew something had to change. I couldn't continue at the same pace, and we needed more structure, oversight and administration if we were to grow the way God seemed to be leading us. I realized I needed a team of capable leaders to share the leadership load. It was getting too big and complex for Dewi and me—Especially considering the cultural complexities. Developing this program was a huge task. It was critical that we find educated Nusandian leaders who could handle both the modern business requirements of the project and the challenges of working with Kantoli people. It would be easier for them to say "yes" and "no" in a way the

Kantoli could understand. They would know how to respond when someone wanted a higher wage for lousy work, and they could work things out if someone wanted an advance to buy a goat or rabbit.

I started to pray specifically that the Lord would send capable help my way, someone who could take this thing and run with it.

As I recuperated, Steve stayed quite involved and helped to take up much of the slack. He saw tremendous potential in the project and encouraged me from the beginning. I honestly could never have done it without his encouragement. Even though he was busy with a million other responsibilities, he studied the operation and came up with some plans.

Steve figured out that we could streamline the process in order to expand more quickly and help more families. We would need to decentralize our operations and, at the same time, build in some systemization and specialization. Why not use the rented house in the city to assemble prepared packets, complete with pre-cut quilt pieces, patterns, batting and backing? Then we could distribute these packets to cooperatives in villages all over the province. That way the villagers didn't need to leave their homes and come to the city to work. The work could be delivered straight to their locations. Each time someone took packets to a village, he could inspect the items the workers had already completed. They would be compensated for the finished products, which would then be brought back to the city for sale.

I thought this was a genius idea. A well-run production hub in the city could provide work for hundreds of people in the rural areas. Trained workers under good supervision could do the cutting and design work. Workers in the cooperatives would need to be trained only in the art of hand stitching. Each village or cooperative could even specialize in unique quilt patterns.

With the new, expanded vision in mind, we constructed more quilting tables and placed them in two villages—Banteng and Pangon—where we trained many hand-sewers. So many people wanted to get involved that we were forced to turn many away. Each location chose a leader to serve as their representative and contact person for coordinating communication and deliveries with the production hub—the rented house in the city.

Completely unrelated to our work with HeartCraft, Steve was developing a good friendship with a local Christian businessman named Simon, who owned a couple of garment factories in Denalia. One day he invited Steve and me to have lunch with him and his wife, Lydia, at their factory. I was glad to have this opportunity, as I had never seen any of the factories in the southern part of town. We entered the large warehouse and saw a few hundred people working on sewing machines. I also noticed something else: Scraps of cloth lined the walls of the building. These were leftovers from the jackets that the workers were making.

Over lunch I shared with Simon and Lydia our desire to help the Kantoli people. When the opportunity presented itself, I ventured a question.

"Simon, what do you do with all the scrap cloth that I saw on the sidelines?

"I just get rid of the scraps by throwing them away, or sometimes the poor want to stuff their mattresses with it," he replied.

I could hardly restrain myself. "Would you be interested in donating your leftover fabric to a group of industrious people who are working in my home?"

"What are these people doing in your home?" he asked. "Who are they, and where are they from?"

"They're making patchwork quilts from pieces of cloth. They're finding employment in my home, and I am selling the quilts."

Simon was amazed. "This must be a hobby of yours?"

"No, I actually have never made a quilt before in my life. But God is doing an amazing thing. I know I need to help these people. This is more than a hobby. It's a calling!"

Simon seemed a bit confused as to how a non-quilter could be teaching dozens of unskilled people how to quilt, but as I explained it all, he and Lydia started to understand what was going on.

As a Chinese Nusandian, Simon faced a cultural gap with the Muslim majority. In Nusandia the Chinese generally hold the money because they work hard and they work smart. Education is very important to them, and they often send their kids to private schools or even outside the country for better education.

Simon himself had studied electrical engineering at California State University in Fresno. As a committed and very generous Christian, he was eager to overcome some of the prejudices and barriers that so often hinder the spread of the gospel. He recognized that HeartCraft was doing just that. With a smile, he agreed to give me as many sacks of scrap cloth as I could possibly use! He was delighted to do so; in fact, he said it was an answer to his prayers. He, too, had specifically been praying for an opportunity to be a blessing.

Before I could thank him, Simon went a step further. He offered to supply us with huge rolls of Dacron padding at wholesale cost! I could hardly believe it. Simon's factory produced winter jackets for export to Holland, the United Kingdom and

164

other parts of Europe. The padding they used was exactly the same thickness that we needed to make good quilts. Simon knew where to get this padding in large volumes at a wholesale price. He also offered to deliver it right to our door.

Simon shows us his factory.

That afternoon I returned home with a happy heart. Once again, God was performing miracles to bless our effort. It sure was nice to be working hand in hand with God!

I couldn't wait to tell Dewi what had happened. Tears welled up in her eyes as I related my story. She knew this meant more cloth and more jobs for more people. Silently, I was adding one more important element—more opportunities for people to hear the life-changing message of God's love for them.

"Doesn't all this sound familiar to you?" Steve asked me later that night. "A wealthy man giving the leftovers from his business to the poor, to help them survive in difficult times?"

"It sure does," I replied without hesitation. "It's the Old Testament story of Ruth and Boaz!"

I knew the story well. It is found in the 3,000-year-old book of Ruth, one of my favorite books of the Bible. Boaz instructed his workmen not to pick up any of the wheat that they dropped during the harvest process. The gleaners would gather it and live off it. Ruth and Naomi were among the gleaners. In fact, this was a part of Jewish law: "When you are harvesting your crops and forget to bring in a bundle of grain from your field, don't go back to get it. Leave it for the foreigners, orphans, and widows. Then the Lord your God will bless you in all you do" (Deuteronomy 24:19).

It was a reflection of God's heart for the poor. Our friend Simon was a modern-day Boaz, deliberately giving his surplus so that the poor could have jobs. For the growing HeartCraft family, his generosity made a huge difference.

An employee sorting fabric scraps

We needed a way to process the new donations of scraps. Dewi quickly organized the workers into groups. A few ladies were trained in how to sort the free scraps into piles by color. The men would then cut and machine-stitch the pieces together.

The women in the villages would do the hand quilting on the tops of quilts.

As usual, we faced additional challenges. Some of them were even a little humorous. One major challenge was quality control. How were we going to keep the quilts clean? We were no longer making the quilts in the rented house in town; now they were being made in far-away mountain villages where they had to be laid out on the floor while workers fastened together the top, batting, and bottom. At any time, someone might sit or walk on the quilts. One of Dadang's quilts, for example had brown hoof prints on it—the result of a goat marching across it.

Other quilts had obvious cigarette holes in them, even though Dewi and I repeatedly forbade the men from smoking near the quilts. Almost all Nusandian men smoke; it's a show of manliness. "Marlboro Man" billboards are ubiquitous.

Still other quilts had tea and coffee stains on them. The island produces fantastic coffee, and the entire country loves tea and coffee. In the process of sewing on the machine or quilting, someone could easily spill a cup of tea or coffee. Worse still, the hot sauce from lunch might get on the quilt. Sometimes the pins that we used to hold the fabric together would rust in the humidity. Or the ladies who quilted would prick themselves with a needle and bleed on the quilt. Rust and blood were some of the most difficult stains to remove. We wrote friends in the States and asked them to send stain removers, but we never seemed to have an adequate supply.

We established some rules and tried to drive them home. There was to be no smoking near the quilts or materials or scraps. Men must exit the building if they needed to smoke. Nor was there to be any eating near the quilts. If the quilts were returned dirty, we would pay less because we had to spend a lot of time washing and cleaning them.

Another problem confronted me. The selvage or edges of the uncut cloth would often include the printed words, "100 percent cotton." The quilters were delighted to see these English words. They assumed that because these words were English, they were sophisticated and important. They thought the words looked nice and figured I'd think so too, since it was my language. So they didn't cut off the words; instead they put them in the middle of the quilts. I'll never forget the day I saw the words "100% cotton" right smack dab in the middle of a Texas-star quilt. I almost fainted. It was a beautifully done quilt, but there in the middle were those unsightly words. To the quilter these words were things of beauty and deserved to be the focal point of the quilt!

Some of the quilters Linda Bauman trained gave her a quilt.

I had long ago learned that it was better for me not to correct the workers myself, but rather to give my opinions to Dewi and let her handle things in a Kantoli way. This saved me a lot of time. She was a master at it, and it didn't seem to drain her as much as it did me. I loved the people and didn't want to offend anyone, but I was impatient and wanted things to move forward quickly without compromising quality.

It was all part of our growing pains. It seemed like every time I wanted things to go better or more smoothly, something would happen. It was a constant process of going a few steps forward and then a few steps back.

Two other major challenges we faced were the need for training and diversification. If we really wanted to do a better job and see this entire program reach a new level, we needed better training for our workers, and we needed to diversify the patterns. We had to get beyond squares, fans, and stars. Dewi and I were exhausting our creative resources. Frankly, my own knowledge and quilting skills were severely limited. How could our workers get the training they needed? I certainly wasn't going to be able to take them any further myself.

❁

Jan Casey, my friend and mentor, met a woman who was an expert quilter. Linda Bauman lived in Colorado, and her quilts had won awards. Photos of her quilts even appeared in quilting magazines. When Jan told her about HeartCraft, Linda wondered if she might be of some help to us in Nusandia. I challenged her to come out and help me move the quality of our quilts to a new level. Linda was delighted. She had long wondered how the Lord might someday use her talent in quilting. We both recognized this was a divine connection and a strategic time for her to come—yet another thread in God's plan.

Before she departed the U.S., Linda went to work creating samples from her own scraps of cloth in her sewing room. She sold some of her beautiful quilts to pay for the ticket to Nusandia, and she spread the word so that people would be praying for her.

Linda arrived in March 1993. I enjoyed her tremendously from the moment I met her. I was only weeks away from delivering my third baby, and it was difficult for me to move quickly and stand on my feet all day, but I had to. Linda was going to be with me for only three weeks.

When she came, I unloaded on Linda all of my quilting challenges. She was ready to help! My job was to be the translator. We brainstormed about the best way to arrange a training program. When word got out that an expert quilter had come from America to provide training, news spread like wildfire. Although every one of the quilters wanted to come, we felt it best to select the top twenty most skilled quilters. Later, they in turn would be able to train others.

We set up big tables so that Linda could spread out her demonstrations. We got machines ready. We had an ironing board and cloth for her to use. We planned which patterns we would try to conquer each day. Dewi organized the trainees into groups. Dewi would have loved to be a trainee herself, but like me she was too busy managing the process. I was the translator, and doing this all day every day for three weeks was hard work (especially being eight months pregnant). I was going on adrenaline so much that I did not see how my feet were swelling, but there was no time to sit and rest until evening.

Linda came with amazing samples. Some of her ideas were beautiful yet simple to do. Still other samples were more for intermediate quilters. Then there were patterns for the expert quilters, such as appliqué. These required much more work and skill than a patchwork quilt.

Linda also brought tools that were not yet available in Nusandia: rotary cutters, cutting mats and rulers—things we'd never seen. To the people, it seemed like Linda could work magic. She could take strips of cloth, sew them together, and then cut them on the diagonal, and they would make a Texas-star quilt. She taught us speed-quilting techniques. I will never forget the day when she taught everyone the Texas star, and they realized it wasn't so hard after all. They were already stitching the Texas star, but it was taking them so long because they didn't know the trick of cutting and sewing the pieces in long strips, rather than little piece by little piece. They didn't know the short cuts. The appliqué projects would be ideal for ladies who needed smaller projects to take home with them. The wedding-ring quilt was a challenge with its scalloped edge, but this too they managed to conquer in short order. The wedding rings we had attempted in the past did not turn the corners nicely. We were on a roll!

I was sad to see Linda go when her three weeks were over. She had accomplished more than she would ever know. The designs she taught the HeartCraft workers would be repeated thousands of times over in years to come. If ever there was an American woman who made an impact on a short trip overseas, it was Linda.

A week after Linda flew home to America, I delivered my third baby girl, Kelly Ruth. Kelly was a beautiful, big baby—nine pounds, eight ounces. She came rather easily, in just a few hours, although the medical staff broke her collarbone in the process. My mother arrived a few days before Kelly was born. Mom always liked to be with me when I was having a baby—not only because she was the proud grandmother, but because she knew I needed the encouragement and help. She knew I'd be giving birth in a rudimentary developing-world clinic and that I could use the companionship.

I was always amused at how the nurses would ask me if I wanted to take the placenta home after I'd given birth. In traditional Kantoli culture, one normally takes the placenta home and buries it in the back yard for good luck. Shortly after Kelly was born, an article appeared in the paper, stating that the authorities had nabbed 300 cats in the city's main public hospital compound. Most of them, the article said, were found outside the maternity ward near the garbage cans where the nurses would toss the placentas if the mothers did not want to keep them! The cats were feasting on the placentas. The officers rounded up the cats and let them go in distant parts of the city. Because the prophet Mohammed had a cat, cats are protected and greatly outnumber dogs in many Muslim cities.

Kelly and Eti

While my mother was visiting us, Steve heard about a good home that was for rent a few miles further up the mountainside where the air was a bit cooler and cleaner. The house was about the same size as ours, with three small bedrooms, but less expensive. Steve felt it might be wise to move a little farther away from the HeartCraft headquarters so that I would not burn myself out. I agreed that we needed some space. Just a day after Kelly was born, we moved to a house farther up the slope of the volcano.

Steve and I always seemed to do things quickly. Certainly, just days after a baby is born is usually not the time a family decides to move, but that didn't deter us. The opportunity was too good to pass up. Besides, my mother was here. She would be a tremendous help. So on moving day, Steve and Mom mobilized all the quilters to become movers! We had lots of friends helping us. It was obvious they were not professional movers. My mother laughed when she saw one of the men carry a fork from the kitchen to the pick-up truck. I had just delivered Kelly, so I simply sat there and told people what to do. That afternoon, when the baby and I arrived at the new house, there was a big pile of things on the floor, but in a few hours we were all organized and ready for a good night's sleep—except that I had a newborn to feed all night long.

The next day we decided to make the house brighter by knocking out the back wall and putting in a screened porch. The landlord seemed excited for any improvements we would make to the house, as long as it was done at our own expense rather than his. One man came with a small hammer and just kept pounding on the wall for hours, trying to knock it down. Steve finally told him to speed things up by using a sledgehammer. Mom thought this was really funny. The Kantoli are rarely in a rush. They have lots of time and appear to have very few goals in life. The longer a project takes, the longer the pay is likely to last.

The repairs were a big help. The house had a lot of mildew, and the previous residents had been sick a lot. By opening the house to sunlight and fresh air, we were able to get rid of the mildew. And there was something else I loved about the house; although it was a smaller home than the one we'd moved from, it had a garage. I caught myself thinking, "Perhaps I could have a little quilting group in the garage?"

There was a large mosque right down the street from our new house. It wasn't just any mosque. It was well known in the city as being fairly radical, with an Islamic training school connected to it. Crowds, mostly young people, would go to this mosque daily, especially on Fridays. A thoughtful neighbor took me aside and told me that it might be wise for us not to let our girls play in the front yard for fear of what the extremists down the street might do to the children of the infidels. This surprised me. Previously, I'd not felt any real direct danger from the mosques near our homes. This one seemed a little different, but we decided not to let it bother us.

Joy stands next to the house with the damaged wall.

After we moved in, we immediately set out to get to know our neighbors. This was always a very important first step when moving into a new community. We knew the routine well by now—we'd been through it a couple of times before. The neighbors would also need to get to know us. They would be curious about all of the traffic as people entered and exited our home. A few early explanations from us would go a long way toward preventing wild rumors from spreading through the community.

One day not long after we moved in, we parked our car in our driveway after returning from an errand. The driveway in this house was on a bit of an incline. We applied the emergency break as an extra precaution. An hour or so later, Steve and I heard a terrible noise followed by shouts in the street. We glanced out the window and saw a crowd forming. Steve called out to me, "Look, Arlene, someone drove their car into the neighbor's house, across the street!"

We all went running outside to join the drama that was unfolding in our neighborhood. Sure enough, a car had rammed through the front wall of the neighbors' house into their living room. As we got closer, we realized to our horror that it was our car! Somehow, our old Toyota Corona had rolled backward down our driveway, across the street and right into the home of one of our new neighbors!

We apologized profusely and offered to cover the cost of rebuilding their wall (probably a hundred dollars or so). This was one of our first introductions into this new community—a little crazy to say the least! We were thankful that no one was hurt. It reminded us that we needed to slow down just a little.

Our move was hard for Dewi. She enjoyed my company so much, but I knew it had to be done. As my family was growing, so also was the need to focus on the children. I sensed that if I would trust God and let go, He would take care of this growing group of people.

After the busy pace I'd been keeping, I relished the quiet times alone rocking Kelly. It was fun talking with Mom and catching up on all the things that were happening back home in the U.S.—America seemed so far away now. As usual, Mom was an incredible help. This was her third or fourth visit. Even the immigration officials at the airport seemed to recognize her. Mom was learning some key Nusandian words, like yes, no,

175

good and don't! She became quite good at using sign language to communicate.

We now had three lovely, active girls. They loved life in Nusandia, and the older two had learned a lot of the language. They spoke it naturally with perfect accents. Kelly was an easy baby. Though we soon had some people working in our garage each day, it was good to have some distance between the main production center and us. They wanted more of me, but I felt for the sake of the ministry I needed to teach them independence. If I ever had to leave the country for any reason, they must be able to continue on without me.

Chapter 14

BUSINESS AS BLESSING

Whenever trouble comes your way, let it be an
opportunity for joy. For when your faith is tested, your
endurance has a chance to grow.

—JAMES 1:2 NLT

While God was blessing HeartCraft, he was also adding to our Pioneers team and ministry. By this time we had about 45 international teammates and dozens of exciting programs underway. We all worked together on various aspects of a strategy called Lampstand, masterminded by Roger and Janice Casey and their Nusandian co-workers. By now the Caseys had 30 years of experience working with the Kantoli people.

The name Lampstand is based on Matthew chapter five, in which the Lord instructs His followers not to hide their faith, but to lift the truth high for all to see. We wanted millions of Kantoli who had never met a Christian, much less heard a clear explanation of the gospel, to know that God spoke their language.

Early retreat of Kantoli believers

Lampstand was an effective ministry strategy because it was about the big picture of discipling a whole people group. We liked the idea because it would bring believers together. United, they would have more resilience. When individuals responded in faith to Christ, their lives changed, but in a Muslim society such as in Nusandia, there was typically a strong negative reaction from the community. Islam, unlike Christianity, is a political system and an entire way of life. It does not tolerate an individual stepping out and embracing a different path. For many Muslims, embracing a different faith is considered the worst possible sin—punishable by death. Not surprisingly, new Christians sometimes feared for their very lives. Husbands would beat wives and daughters into submission, and men who identified themselves with Jesus would lose their jobs, be disowned by their families or be thrown out of their communities.

Life-threatening persecution against new believers is sadly a fact of life in cultures like the one we were in. The persecution came in waves and varied in intensity from place to place. In the late 1980s, many young men were being recruited openly in the streets of the capital city. They were sent to the eastern islands to hunt down and kill Christians. It saddened me that many people in America and the West didn't seem to notice or care about the persecution of Christians in other countries. Why is it that most people only notice injustice when it affects them directly? If we don't extend a helping hand to Christians in other lands, I thought to myself, this kind of Muslim persecution could eventually affect people in the West.

One of the goals of Lampstand was to give these new believers, who were considered outcasts from their own families and communities, a sense of belonging. They would immediately be part of a community where they could receive the support they would need when their friends and relatives abandoned them. A multifaceted strategy, Lampstand involved the development of Kantoli Christian expressions, including language, music, drama, arts, media, community development and theological training. All were intended to foster a broad church-multiplying chain reaction. Our Lampstand team partnered in this effort with as many as 30 Nusandian church denominations, all of which had at least some level of interest in seeing churches started among the 35 million Kantoli people.

As a team, we fully embraced this strategy and worked hard to see all the pieces fall into place. It was quickly evident to us that it was effective. The number of Christ-followers began to multiply rather rapidly, compared to very slow growth in prior years. Although the needs and opportunities remained infinite, we were all filled with hope, unity and expectation of what God was going to do among the Kantoli. It was a special joy for Steve and me to see how individuals who God brought to the team each made a unique and powerful contribution. Some got involved in media, others in training church planters and still others contributed their agricultural, business, educational or health related skills.

HeartCraft was part of the community development and business aspect of the Lampstand strategy. Our ultimate goal was to see churches reproduce and multiply among this Muslim people group. We were motivated by an awareness that God cares for the whole person, not only the soul. Jesus healed the lame, the blind and the sick. He fed the hungry. He met people just where they were, but He never left them the same. He also cared about the simple things in life—like paying taxes and providing quality wine at a wedding.

It was clear to Steve that my primary goal with HeartCraft should be to replace myself. I was busy being a mother of three darling little girls and was very involved in our international team. The days were full. In truth, we needed more than one capable leader for HeartCraft, which by now had become a formalized Nusandian non-profit organization complete with a board of directors. Much of our marketing took place in the capital city, a three-hour drive from where we lived. Dewi and I often travelled there to attend the American Women's Association fairs as well as bazaars held by the Australian and Kiwi (New Zealand) and Japanese expatriate communities. We needed someone who spoke English and could take orders and communicate with customers.

Steve began a careful search for a Nusandian marketing director for HeartCraft. We wanted someone who would honor Dewi and work well with her, but who could take HeartCraft to a level that Dewi could never dream of doing with her limited education. And that's when we found Faith. Faith was a university graduate and the daughter of a Nusandian pastor. When she was a young girl, her family lived in Australia for six years.

There, she had the unique privilege of learning the English language while she was a child, and as a result she was fluent.

Faith came to us when we were at a serious point of need. She was a growing and devoted Christian who had a passion for people. Not only did she speak flawless English, but she was well organized. She wanted to use her marketing skills and was delighted to be able to use these gifts in a non-profit business environment.

Faith made an amazing addition to the team in her new role as marketing director. She didn't let things fall through the cracks. She was great in sales, too. By then we had opened up a small shop on a busy Denalia road—actually in the garage of our close friends from Singapore, Patrick and Catherine. They were our new teammates, and we felt very blessed to have them. We replaced their garage door with a large picture window. A carpenter tiled the floor, built shelves all around the walls to display the quilts and added spotlights on the ceiling. There was not another store like it in all of Nusandia. We got some good traffic there, and it helped put us on the map as a real business. Faith helped with this expansion, offering good suggestions, and she developed the marketing strategy that allowed us to keep growing.

Hasan was another person we interviewed during this time of rapid growth. He, too, was an English speaker who grew up playing with American children near the U.S. oil camps on a nearby island. He was able to complete a few years of university but had to leave school due to a lack of finances.

We liked Hasan. He, too, wanted to be involved in ministry and business. We needed someone who would plan the production line and be a liaison between the village groups and the main production center. Hasan seemed like a perfect fit. We hired him, and Dewi and I began training him to help in production.

Training programs were one of the ways we expanded quickly. We poured ourselves into a few workers, and then they would carry the skills back to the village areas. The training programs were very hard work, but we realized that they were well worth the effort. Some of the men from the Pioneers team began to place Kantoli evangelists and church planters in these programs. They were young men and women who were passionate about reaching the lost in village areas, but they needed income-generating skills. If a believer could provide jobs to the community he was serving, his message would be much more readily received. These young evangelists and church planters knew how important it was to be a blessing in a tangible way.

Kantoli believers using traditional instruments

The number of staff grew even more, and we soon had nearly 200 people who were fully employed with HeartCraft, either in Denalia or the villages. It was fun to see the dedicated Christians mingling with the Muslim quilters. The variety of conversations was something I had never heard before in Denalia. There was a noticeable sense of God's presence among these quilters who had never been exposed to the lives of true believers.

The evangelists used their newfound skills to open unreached areas with the gospel. They started quilting groups and often travelled back and forth to the city of Denalia for supplies— although supplies were not the only things they brought to the villages. They also brought Bibles, the *Jesus* film and a Kantoli-language Christian magazine Steve had developed, called *Visiting Friend,* as well as other videos and literature. When people responded and decided to follow Christ, the evangelists taught them some basics about their new faith, gave them Bibles and helped them to organize small house churches. It was very exciting for me to see how HeartCraft had an instrumental role in this process. God was certainly expanding our borders.

✖

In 1993, Tom and Brenda Hargray and their four children joined our team. It wasn't long before we wondered how we had ever survived without them. Brenda was the daughter of a Cornell University professor. She and Tom had built a successful printing business in the Philadelphia area. Brenda had a good knowledge of business and a heart for the people. She was just what I needed in a friend and co-worker.

The house that we had rented to use as a production center was quite large. In Nusandia, homes are rented by the year rather than by the month. In fact, this house was like two houses, one behind the other. Some of the HeartCraft workers lived in the back part (It wasn't safe to leave a building unoccupied at night.), but there was still extra room in the front section. Tom and Brenda thought it would be an excellent place for them to live as they got started on language and culture learning, so they moved in with their family. They knew it would help them make faster progress in the language if they had Nusandians around them 24/7. That way they could also help subsidize the cost of the house for HeartCraft by paying $500 per year toward the rent.

While Tom got involved in various media projects, Brenda's goal was to work with me in HeartCraft. Even though she was just starting to learn the language, Brenda got plugged in almost immediately. She spent a lot of time organizing the financial side of things and developing the leaders. She was actually good at everything and quickly became a close friend to Faith and the other leaders.

In the back of the house many quilters were working every day. We valiantly tried to keep them outside whenever they smoked, and they would normally take their cigarette breaks on the second-floor balcony behind the house. The ashes from their cigarettes would drift over the rail onto the ground below. When they finished their cigarettes, they'd toss the stubs over the rail.

For a long time, this wasn't a problem because it rained almost every day during the rainy season. Over time, however, there was more and more clutter on the ground below the balcony. When the cutters would sweep up the threads and cloth scraps after their day's work, they would sweep all the fragments out of the back door and off the balcony onto the ground ten or twelve feet below. Why expend energy putting the garbage in a bag or bin, when you can just sweep it out the door?

One day during the dry season, when it rarely rained for several months, someone tossed a cigarette into the pile of old scraps below the porch. This time it caught on fire. Brenda and I were gone, and Tom happened to be home. After one of the smoking breaks, the quilting team smelled smoke. No one paid much attention for a while because in Nusandia it is common to smell smoke. People burn things all the time. Then someone yelled, "Api!" and everyone ran to the balcony to see that the scraps below had erupted in flames. The flames threatened to envelop all of our supplies, the stack of newly-made quilts and the house itself!

Hearing the cries of panic, Tom rushed to the rear of the house and sized up the situation. There was no functional fire department in Denalia, and even if there were, it would take an hour for someone to reach the house through stop-and-go traffic. There was no such thing as fire insurance, either.

Tom grabbed a couple of buckets and moved into action. There is very little water pressure available in most Nusandian homes. Most homes have their own well. Thankfully, Nusandians always have a large tank of water in their bathrooms, which they keep filled all the time. To take a bath, they just use a dipper and pour water over themselves from the tank.

Tom and the men quickly formed a bucket brigade, using the two or three buckets that were available. Others stomped on the flames and tried to smother them with rugs. Miraculously, they were able to bring the fire under control before it spread too far. The outside wall of the house was black, and part of the balcony had been damaged, but that was all. The smoke residue in the house could be washed off the walls and ceilings over time. We were so thankful for the Lord's protection. The incident reminded us of the challenges we faced in this invigorating but oftentimes agonizing work.

Tom and Brenda and their four kids were real troopers and so were the two ladies who helped them in the kitchen. One day while the family was out, two thieves stormed into the house and grabbed the two women who were working in the kitchen. They put sharp knives to their throats. Thankfully, Deki, one of the taller, stronger quilters, was walking from the back house to the front and noticed the two women were in trouble. He called for help and started toward the ladies. Deki was a rough looking man with tattoos and a big mustache, who'd been involved in the local mafia. The thieves took one look at him and decided it wasn't worth the risk. They lowered their knives and made a dash for the door. Tom and Brenda arrived home later and heard the story from all the people in their house. Events like these kept us praying and reminded us how much we needed God's supernatural protection.

Another time one of the quilters went to the ironing table, and, as she lifted a piece of patchwork from the pile, she let out a cry. She had startled a poisonous snake that had been hiding under the fabric. One of the men ran in with a machete and killed it.

Still another time, Dewi and I were organizing the cloth in the storage area when a huge rat jumped out of the big bag of scrap cloth. I was so startled! It wasn't unusual to see rats, but to have one jump out at you was frightening.

We never knew what was going to happen. Sometimes the men coming in from the villages would stay overnight before making the long trip home. One night they heard a leaky faucet in the bathroom. It dripped all night. One of the men started a rumor that there was an evil spirit taking a shower. The rumor passed around from quilter to quilter until we hardly had anyone showing up for work. The evil spirits frightened them. No one wanted to work in a haunted house.

We faced many more challenges far more disturbing than drippy faucets or leaping rats. For example, Faith, Dewi and I became aware that many of our patterns were missing. Dewi and I had a growing suspicion that someone was stealing our patterns and taking them home after work. No one wanted to frisk the workers as they left each evening. We started to be more careful and watch our patterns more closely. Rumor had it that some of the people were putting pieces of cloth and patterns in their underwear!

Eventually we were forced to start checking the workers' bags when they went home, a common practice in Nusandia that we finally had to adopt. As much as we wanted to trust people, we were working in a culture in which trust was a rare commodity. Even though they had benefitted so much from our help, some of the people were stealing from the project.

Sadly, the Christians who were working alongside the Muslims didn't always hold higher standards. One day a huge fight broke out among the men working in the cutting section. Though many of the men were involved, with fists flying, at the center of the melee, were two Christians who were trying to stab each other with scissors. Other men had to pull them apart and calm them down! Thankfully, no one was seriously hurt, although emotions ran very high.

Some people were Christians in name only. Nusandians called them "card-carrying Christians," a reference to the identity card everyone in the country has to carry, which identifies one's religion among other things. The only way you could tell that these particular people were Christians was by their ID cards; their lives didn't show any authentic faith.

Other challenges that were especially difficult related to the banking system and thievery. For example, Faith went to the bank one day to withdraw a lot of money to pay wages and purchase cloth. Everything is done in cash in Nusandia—even buying a car. The amount was substantial. Faith was careful to observe her surroundings as she left the bank. She looked to the right and left. Everything looked fine. She got into the car and headed back to the shop.

Minutes later, the car shook a bit as if it had a flat tire. The driver pulled the car to the side of the road. Quite a few people gathered around and even a couple of motorcycles stopped to see what was happening. The traffic slowed down around them. While the tire was being changed, Faith didn't notice that someone quietly forced a window open and reached into the car. Faith had set the briefcase with the money in it next to her on the seat, to guard it. In just a split second of inattention, it disappeared into the crowd. It was that fast!

In a flash, Faith realized what had happened and jumped out of the car. Sure enough, it was quickly evident that the car tire had been slashed deliberately. It had all been part of a premeditated plan. It was probably a group of young guys who were in on the plan together. Sometimes a teller in the bank will make a quick call to friends waiting outside, letting them know when someone has taken a lot of money out of an account. They will follow the person's car for a distance on a motorcycle, and then come up close and throw some sharp objects on the road so that the car's tires will go flat. Then they'll offer to help change the tire, and while they're doing the work, one of their friends will steal the money from the car. Along with the money they also took Faith's ATM card. They went immediately to the ATM machine and started to get as much money as they could. As soon as the tire was replaced, Faith raced quickly back to the bank in order to have them suspend her ATM card. Unfortunately, more money had already been lost.

On another occasion, Steve went to the bank to withdraw several thousand dollars worth of money to pay a couple of year's rent on the building and to purchase a large amount of cloth from Simon, the factory owner. On the way back, Steve stopped at a friend's house. He needed to run into the house for two or three minutes to get something before driving on to his destinations, where he would deliver the funds. The money was stacked in two large envelopes. Rather than carry it with him into the house, he placed one envelope in the glove compartment and the other under the front driver's seat. Then he locked the car and went into the house.

When Steve returned to the car less than five minutes later, he noticed the car door was not locked. Had he forgotten to lock it? Sure enough, when he reached into the glove compartment, the envelope with three thousand dollars in it had vanished. Then he reached under the seat and saw that the second envelope with the other half of the money was still there! The thieves had worked swiftly to get into the car as soon as he'd parked in the driveway. They'd been following him from a distance, watching for an opportunity. They'd only had time to find the one envelope, not the other. How saddened we were by the loss, and yet we were thankful that God had spared the second half. We were learning rather quickly how serious the thievery problem could be and how the tricks of the trade work.

Crimes like these caused great headaches for our small but growing work. Everywhere we turned it seemed like we were having money stolen. This was hard earned money, and it hurt. And, if it was not money that was stolen, it would be our patterns, cloth or our sanity! Sometimes we wondered if it was worth it, but we felt the Lord saying we should persevere.

Chapter 15

A BROKEN NOSE

Oh the joys of those who are kind to the poor.
The Lord rescues them in times of trouble.

—PSALM 41:1 NLT

In late 1993, our family was ready for a second visit back to the U.S. We had been in Nusandia for seven years. It was hard for me to leave but reassuring to know that Brenda, Patrick and Catherine would be there to help the small team of HeartCraft leaders who oversaw the 200 employees.

Brenda and I talked about where things stood. We both agreed that HeartCraft had reached a plateau and needed some strategic, structural changes if it was to move into a new level of impact and fruitfulness. One key, we thought, would be to hire someone responsible for the spiritual aspects of HeartCraft—a kind of chaplain. After all, we weren't just trying to meet people's physical needs. We wanted to see them freed from destructive cultural patterns and spiritual bondage as well. We knew it would be best to find a Nusandian, or better yet a Kantoli, to fill this role.

Another important role that needed to be filled was someone to serve as director of the entire program—a CEO for the organization. Until now this role had been filled by several of us working as a team. It was time for us to have a clear Nusandian leader.

While we were in the U.S. for six months, Steve and I got word from Brenda that she had located and hired two top-notch people who could fill these slots. What great news! One of them, Amir, was due to graduate from the university and would be available soon. He would make an excellent director for Heart-Craft. A sharp English speaker with a degree in business, Amir was a Christian Nusandian from another island.

The other new hire was a Kantoli man named Rohandi. He was an elder in a Kantoli congregation, and he was enthusiastic and gregarious—just what we needed to oversee the spiritual aspects of our work. Rohandi's wife, Lena, was also personable. Both appeared to have a clear desire to serve their own people, and I was eager to work with them when I returned to Denalia.

After five months in the U.S., we flew back to Nusandia, and it was exciting to be back in the middle of things. I was pleased and thankful to meet Amir, Rohandi and Lena. I liked them all. We had navigated many difficult transitions and trials, and it would be good to have reliable leaders at the helm.

Steve and I attended Amir's graduation—amazed that we would have a director who was a graduate with a degree in business. We began to work with Amir and pour ourselves into him. He seemed to understand exactly what needed to be done.

Rohandi, too, became very busy making constant trips out into the village areas. His job was to take all the work packets to the groups outside the city, pick up completed orders, and at the same time, encourage the groups spiritually. The momentum started accelerating again.

For greater efficiency, we followed Steve's advice and expanded the cutting division of the business. By doing this and focusing on marketing, we could enroll more workers. Steve met regularly for Bible study with the men of the cutting team. It was exciting to see their eyes open as they read and discussed various passages of Scripture.

One day Steve and I were in our van going somewhere and witnessed a motorcycle accident—a hit and run. A young man lay motionless in the middle of the road and obviously needed help. We jumped out, put him into our car and quickly drove him to the nearest hospital. We waited until he regained consciousness, which wasn't a long time, so perhaps he'd had a minor concussion. He was extremely grateful for our unsolicited help. He was unemployed, and the doctor's bill was going to cost him more than he was able to pay. Steve and I glanced at each other, and I suggested that he interview at HeartCraft.

Shortly after he healed from his injuries, this young man became a part of the cutting team and eventually embraced Christ as his Savior. Events like this were constant reminders of God's presence and direction. He gave us many divine appointments that we could never have arranged for ourselves.

Rohandi went to work assembling and distributing packages of quilts that had the patterns and directions clearly spelled out on the front. He became fast and efficient, although we also began to see another side to his personality. Sadly he often clashed with Dewi and the other leaders. We started to get complaints from the villagers and other staff about Rohandi's style.

He loved to boss people around and give orders. Various visitors from the cooperatives would share their disappointments about Rohandi's visits. Something was going wrong. If he had been hired to be a pastor and spiritual counselor to these quilting groups, this certainly was not being accomplished. In fact, he was having an opposite effect. I pondered these things, and we tried to help Rohandi soften his approach.

In some ways I really liked Rohandi. His style was similar to what would be expected in an American working environment. He called things as he saw them. The only problem was, we were not in America, and we needed someone with a humble attitude to deal with the people in the villages. People were getting uneasy and resentful. Many aspects of the work were in turmoil, and Rohandi's heavy-handed approach wasn't helping matters.

�֊

During this time of growth, the Lord added once again to our Pioneers team. Dean and Jane Chester and their four children joined us. Dean had been a pastor for several years in upstate New York, so this couple came with considerable life experience. While some expressed concern about the potential difficulty of their adjustment as a larger family with older children, Steve and I felt it was worth the risk.

On their arrival, the Chesters immediately plunged into the culture and language. They deliberately chose a home in a relatively poor and very populated area, even though it had water problems and was located right next to a cemetery. From the upstairs window, there was a clear view of the Islamic cemetery.

"Jane, why did you pick such a radical place to live?" I asked.

"The cemetery reminds us of why we are here," she replied. "Besides, this community is so tight. It will force us to learn the language faster."

What a remarkable family they were. And God even brought to HeartCraft our very own expert quilter. Jane had done it all! She not only knew the art of quilting, but she was also a mathematician. We were having some trouble making our patterns work, but in no time at all, Jane standardized all of the patterns and created new ones for us. She had great ideas for design and color combinations at a time when I was moving ahead in other areas of the work.

Jane even made patterns out of hard plastic sheets to replace the old cardboard ones that wore out so quickly. Everything became more accurate. Jane helped the staff create new quilt concepts based on authentic Nusandian batik cloth and designs. These new designs were stunning. Because she lived right up the road, it was like having a Linda Bauman available to us all the time. Jane was able to stop in frequently to check the quality of the work.

By this time we had totally outgrown our little garage store and really needed space for a showroom. We found it on the ground floor of a new building that our friend Simon was constructing. The building was big enough to house our team's English Institute, Simon's personal offices, a conference and prayer room and offices for Steve and some of his staff. The building had four floors, and the ground floor became a showroom for a HeartCraft store. What an incredible provision from the Lord! We were blown away by Simon's generosity and vision for ministry. He was a Boaz to us once again.

❀

Not long after the big new store opened for business, Jane came to visit with new ideas, samples and her usual word of encouragement. As she was leaving the store I saw her walk toward the big plate-glass wall at the front of the showroom. It actually looked like there was nothing there at all. The glass had only recently been installed, and we had not yet put any props or furniture near the window. Jane obviously didn't realize it was there, and she walked right into it. Suddenly, there was a loud bang. She fell backward and hit the ground, blood spurting from her nose. She had clearly broken it. The HeartCraft driver and I quickly scooped her up and rushed her off in the van to the hospital.

Our first showroom in Denalia

Being the cheerful person that she was, on the way to the hospital, Jane commented that God must have a purpose in it all, just like when she arrived in Nusandia and a motorcycle ran over her foot and broke it. I didn't know whether to laugh or cry. Jane was such a wonderful person. Why did these kinds of things keep happening to her?

We drove to the emergency room as quickly as we could, only to wait for a long, long time in a line of sick and suffering people. Everything seemed to move in slow motion at the hospital. I wondered why they even called it an emergency room. Finally, after what seemed like years, they ushered us in. I explained that my friend had broken her nose and needed help. The doctor seemed more interested in the story of *how* Jane broke her nose than in doing something about it. Finally, he took a flashlight and shined it up her nose.

"It will be fine," he said, switching off the light. "She just stunned it in the accident. Take a couple of aspirin, and go home for rest.

"What?" I said, rapidly losing patience with this man. "You have got to be kidding!"

In her sweet and calm voice, Jane told him, "But, Sir, I can move my nose around on my face. It is very loose and has never been this way before."

The doctor insisted we were overreacting and told us to relax. We went back out into the waiting room, and I felt very frustrated. What could I do for Jane? She was obviously in pain. Just then I saw a sign on a wall. Just what we were looking for: an ear, nose and throat specialist! I pulled Jane behind me and marched toward the office. I'm sure I startled the nurses when we barged into the office, but it was time for action, and I wasn't going to wait any more.

"Someone help us!" I called out. "My friend has broken her nose, and she's in pain." They got the message and quickly ushered us into the doctor's office.

The specialist shined a flashlight into Jane's nose again. "She has broken her nose," he announced. He sent Jane away to be x-rayed while I waited for the news. After a long time, the x-rays came back, and sure enough, Jane's nose was broken, not only in one place but in three places. In fact it was swelling rapidly, and she did not look like the same person. The nurses prepared her briefly for surgery, and she was taken out of my sight. When I called her husband, Dean, to tell him Jane was in surgery, he was not surprised by it all and was cheerful just like Jane was. It seemed that Dean and Jane were always cheerful, no matter what happened.

Jane had a special splint on her face for a few weeks. She was hardly recognizable, but the cast did not deter her from returning to HeartCraft and working with the quilters. In fact, she used her extra rest time to make a large, beautiful quilt with Bible verses on it. Each embroidered square was unique and gorgeous.

I thought about the old saying, "When life gives you scraps, make quilts." That was Jane!

It wasn't long before Jane was right back in the groove. Both Brenda and Jane were using their gifts to pour into the staff members while also giving them total room and freedom to make decisions and to grow this ministry. Our role was to be in the background. Faith also showed herself to be quite impressive. She was gifted not only in sales but also in administration and production. When she had suggestions, she would give them to Rohandi and to Amir. They were not always receptive to her good suggestions, however, and seemed to feel threatened by Faith.

Lula, another teammate, and I decorated the store until it was a fabulous showroom. It was a privilege to work with Lula. She had a knack for color and design, and I would just do whatever she said. It wasn't long before the showroom became well known and people came from all over the country to see it. It was a happening place, and sales were strong.

We tried to market the crafts and products every way that we could. First I went up to the oil camps in Sumatra. I shipped huge bags of quilts ahead of me and set up an exhibition for the "captive" American women at the oil camps. They were bored, had lots of money and were more than happy to shop! We would sell about $10,000 worth of quilts on each visit—a lot of money to us.

It was exciting watching all this growth—yet underneath it all I sensed a growing tension. Although I could not immediately put my finger on it, I sensed that something was quite wrong at HeartCraft. On the outside, we looked like a thriving business, but inside lots of rumors were flying. Finally, we realized there was a crisis—in fact, there were three of them. They were all going on at the same time and were about to converge.

First, Hasan was quite sick with tuberculosis. We were helping him out by paying his medical bills. To complicate matters, we learned he was using his wages to set up a competing quilting group on the side! One of his relatives, who worked at Heart-Craft, would take our patterns home in the evenings to train their workers. Needless to say, I was saddened when I found out. But I didn't have time to handle this crisis because there was another: Every day there were more and more complaints about Rohandi offending the villagers. Rather than being a blessing to them and an example of Christ's love, he was actually a poor example. He seemed to be using his position to throw his weight around in an offensive way. He was also in a power struggle with Amir, Faith and Dewi.

As if that wasn't enough, our bookkeeper, Yani, began to notice something over several months: a steady leak of money. One day she realized it was not just a small leak, but a big one. As much as $10,000 had been siphoned out of HeartCraft over a period of about six months. Yani and Brenda pored over the books to be sure and to determine where the money was going. Someone decided to pay a surprise visit to Amir's small home and saw in his modest place a lot of expensive electronics. Amir was the director of HeartCraft at the time. He had a healthy salary but certainly not enough to buy all this equipment. For weeks, Amir had been telling us remarkable stories about dying relatives, medical bills and other mishaps for which he needed money. We'd given him some helpful pay advances, but none of these stories could be verified. We trusted him. What we hadn't realized was that he was pilfering a lot of extra money from HeartCraft on the side.

What were we going to do? Our leaders were self destruct-ing, one by one. Hasan was financing a competitor, Rohandi was undermining morale and Amir was embezzling money. All were serious cases, and their Muslim co-workers were observ-ing their behavior closely. During this time, we also lost a few villages due to some of the Muslim groups wanting to start their own effort. They convinced people to join them with promises of higher wages. These were people I had poured much time and effort into. I felt betrayed and had to lean on the Lord's strength.

After much prayer and thought, Steve advised that we take decisive action. Radical surgery was needed. Though in Nusan-dian culture it was rarely done for fear of a possible backlash, we dismissed Hasan, Rohandi and Amir in rapid succession.

They were painful days for us. Each of these individuals was my personal friend, but each had abused the privilege of leader-ship in this thriving ministry. If anything, Christians needed to measure up to a higher standard than the world around them because people are always looking for opportunities to dis-credit them. Despite the cost and possible reaction, we saw this as a critical test of what HeartCraft was all about—and quite possibly a matter of survival.

Hasan became angry and very hurt. Rohandi threatened to take out a lawsuit against HeartCraft. Amir threatened to report various foreigners to immigration on trumped up charges or to expose the project to the Muslim community. We committed it all to prayer and trusted the Lord for His protection. There wasn't a lot that we could do beyond this. We braced ourselves and kept on pressing forward. Steve's advice was just to lay low, pray and keep our hand to the plow. We did, and it paid off.

As days and weeks passed, nothing cataclysmic happened. Gradually, a fresh breeze began to blow through HeartCraft. We had been willing to see the whole thing collapse rather than leave corrupt or immature leaders in charge. God had miraculously preserved the work. Gossip and rumors started to subside. Emotions healed. Joy and laughter returned.

Faith became HeartCraft's new leader. Of all the staff, she was clearly the most consistent and reliable. We had thought that to be culturally appropriate we needed a man to be in charge, but God wanted a woman for the task. Faith didn't ask to be the new leader. Just as Moses was a reluctant leader, Faith didn't really want the top position, but she was willing to do it. In the days and months ahead we found out just how wonderful a leader she really was. In the midst of all the trauma and change, God gave Steve and me a peace and a sense that He was in control. We prayed more for each other and for the ministry. In my relationship with Dewi, it opened up opportunities for us to talk about standards of integrity and the effects of sin. She was definitely making the connections in her mind.

During these tough times I was encouraged by Psalm 126:5-6: "Those who plant in tears will harvest with shouts of joy. They weep as they go to plant their seed, but they sing as they return with the harvest." These words certainly seemed applicable to our situation. James 1:2-4 has a similar message: "Whenever trouble comes your way, let it be an opportunity for joy. For when your faith is tested, your endurance has a chance to grow. So let it grow, for when your endurance is fully developed, you will be strong in character and ready for anything."

The Lord gave the HeartCraft team and me the strength to persevere. If I had given up, we would have had to close down everything. The pain and tears were a part of the process. I was completely dependent on the Lord, and I knew His grace would be sufficient.

Chapter 16

DOLLS TO REACH AN ISLAND

- - - - - - - -

Don't just pretend that you love others. Really love them.

—ROMANS 12:9 NLT

On the heels of a season of testing and pain, Tati and Lili came into my life. Maybe the Lord knew I needed a reminder that He was still powerfully at work. These two sisters had heard about HeartCraft from one of the employees at Simon's garment factory. Their story immediately caught my attention.

Tati and Lili were from a small Hindu people group hidden in the volcanic highlands in the eastern part of the island, hundreds of miles away. Their tribal group had resisted the advance of Islam centuries earlier. To this day, thousands of them maintain their own animistic and Hindu culture high in the mountain valleys surrounding a spectacular volcanic caldera.

The sisters' father was a Hindu leader. Wanting to keep his family intact, he told his teenage girls never to read the Christian holy book. If they did, he warned them, bad things would happen. His dire predictions only served to excite their curiosity. They wondered if they would ever have a chance to see and hold a Bible.

A few years later, the girls obtained a copy of the Scriptures from some people travelling through the area. Secretly, they began to read it together. The stories, and especially the character of Christ, captivated them. Reading about His life, teaching and sacrifice for them on the cross, the two sisters decided they wanted to become followers of Jesus. The more they read the Bible, the more their lives changed. It was obvious for all to see.

When their father found out, he was furious. He sent them to a Hindu school on a distant island to be deprogrammed from their new Christian thoughts and beliefs. Once again, his plan had the opposite effect. Tati and Lili began leading other young women to faith in Christ. Word of what was happening eventually reached their parents back home. That was the final straw. Their father promptly expelled them from the family.

"You're no longer mine," he told them. "You're on your own. Don't come back here again."

With nowhere else to go, Tati and Lili fled many days' journey to our province. This is how they finally found their way to my home. Finishing their heartrending story, they asked me a straightforward question: "Can you find a place for us in HeartCraft?"

By this time we were making as many as 200 quilted products each month. We seemed to be saturating the national and local markets. It didn't make sense to produce even more. Yet, these two precious women obviously needed help. The words of Scripture flashed through my mind, "Do not withhold good from those who deserve it, when it is in your power to act" (Proverbs 3:27). It would be great to come up with a new product that the sisters could take back to their home area someday, if they ever had a chance to return there.

Our close friend and teammate Karen took Tati and Lili under her wing. Karen made no claims of being a "crafty" kind of person. While she appreciated crafts, she was not one to sit down and use a sewing machine or come up with a new idea. She even claimed that her stick figures needed help! She was more interested in the people side of things. She was willing to do whatever it took to make these precious young women independent and self supporting. She found them a place to live, and they quickly became like daughters to her. Together we began to pray that their father, mother and family would one day come to know Christ.

In the meantime, the sisters worked out of my garage and began to pioneer a new division of HeartCraft. We realized we needed smaller items to sell. Many customers came into the shop needing a small gift for someone and were not willing to buy a big quilt for $100 or $200. I thought that if we had smaller quilted items we could also employ more people—needy people. The time was right for this.

Karen and I made a good team. God had given us a new project—and with it some new territory and a different people group hundreds of miles away. Could it be that HeartCraft would expand beyond the work among the Kantoli to help other ethnic groups on other islands? What a thrill that would be!

As we were thinking and praying about these things, God brought Deki to my mind. Deki, the man who had frightened off the thieves a few months earlier, was a gifted tailor. Deki worked out of his home. In his past, he had been a really rough guy, covered with scars and tattoos. Deki told us he had not been able to make ends meet with his little shop, so he was shutting it down. He needed more steady work, rather than an occasional order for a dress or pair of pants. Deki had exactly the kind of skills we needed—a man who was not afraid of a machine and actually came to us with the skill already in his pocket! He was not only good; he was great.

I knew Deki could figure out how we could make our own small products and patterns. He was not afraid to experiment and try new things. Whatever the concept, he could probably figure out how to do it.

Suddenly, it all came together. I showed Deki a doll that I had purchased at a craft boutique in the U.S. Amazingly, I was able to locate the women who actually made the original doll. I wrote to them and received their permission, no strings attached, to make as many of the dolls as we wanted. They loved the story that I had shared with them, relating what God was doing right in my home. They were eager to see their doll become a blessing to help many poor people. They wrote me a very kind letter and said it would be a great honor for them to have HeartCraft workers make their doll—even in the thousands.

Deki studied the doll and took it apart piece by piece to see how it was made.

He went to work planning the body of the doll and actually created a better pattern than the original. He purchased glue and wool for the hair and gathered scraps from the larger quilts to make little dresses for the doll. Then he got the leftover padding from the larger quilts and stuffed the body of the doll.

The result was a beautiful doll that we playfully called the "Grace doll." It was a reminder, after all we'd been through, that God's grace had reached down and protected us.

But Deki wasn't finished. He took all his skill and carefully transferred it to Tati and Lili. We found we could make the dolls almost completely from leftover cloth from the quilting. Costs were minimal, and they sold at a great price. Before long, the women were making a reasonable living for themselves.

Once again my home became a beehive of activity, but this time it was more under control. We kept almost all the craft work in the garage area. At noon each day, we would share the food with the gang in the garage. I was glad things were relatively under control because, by this time, I was expecting my fourth baby.

The noon meal—a highlight of every day

We all spent long hours in the garage together. Deki was quite a character. He had long hair and a rough look, but he was skilled and had a colorful personality. On a spiritual level, Steve spent time with Deki telling him about the Lord, and he was very open. He didn't make any pretense of being a strong Muslim, like so many. He understood the concept of sin. It was obvious to everyone that he had been a gangster and not a religious man.

The more I worked with Tati and Lili, the more I recognized what remarkable young women they really were. I loved them! They were such companions to me right within my own home.

Around the time that we began making the dolls, a church from Los Angeles sent a large team to work with us for a few weeks. Steve and our eight-year-old daughter, Joy, led them on an exploratory trip to an island called Baskara. As far as we know, Joy was the first little foreign girl ever to visit this island. Steve was hoping that God would somehow open up a way for the 80,000 people on that island to receive the gospel. To reach the island, our team had to sail on an old World War II-era ship. Karen, who had long been burdened for this island, joined them. She had read an article that Steve published after his first visit to the island years earlier. After reading the article, Karen had sensed a call from God to leave her Southern California life and come to Nusandia. She wanted to be a part of reaching Baskara Island for Christ.

It wasn't long after that exploratory trip to Baskara that Karen became convinced the time had come for her to move to a city that was closer to the burden of her heart. During her time in Denalia, she had learned the language well. She was ready to go. As she shared the needs of Baskara with her friends Tati and Lili, they listened intently. They, too, became captured by the vision. The three of them decided to move together to a location not far from the girls' home. They would use this town as a base for reaching Baskara. Since the Grace dolls were a best seller, we knew Tati and Lili could keep making them, even from their new home hundreds of miles away.

Before the young women returned to their home area, God did a miracle. A Nusandian pastor of the church they joined decided to visit their father and share the gospel with him. He traveled way up the mountain valleys to find the old patriarch.

It took a lot of boldness as their father was a leader in the village. God honored the pastor's obedience. After a long discussion, the pastor led the girls' father to faith—and he in turn led his entire family to Christ.

When we got news of this miracle, there was a lot of celebration. God had done the impossible; love had found a way. Tati and Lili were welcomed back into their family, and the pastor made repeated visits to encourage the new believers in their faith. The young women, too, began to teach their father and other family members the basics of the Christian faith.

And they kept making the dolls. Through the income generated from the dolls, they were able to pay their tuition to a local Bible training school. At that training school they both met young Christian men and got married.

But the story doesn't stop there. With Karen's help and mentoring, the sisters and their husbands made survey trips to the island of Baskara. Lili's husband had experience as a baker. His parents had run a bakery for years, and he was a master of the trade. He opened a bakery on the island called "Bread of Life" in their language. Lili kept doing what she had been doing all along—making dolls. Yet this time she was doing it on an island where people watched their every move. Westerners could never have survived there, much less effectively shared the message of Christ.

The story of how these two young ladies became God's channel of blessing to two unreached people groups warrants a book of its own. The sisters and their husbands are my heroes. The simple little Grace doll that was made in my garage was used by God to bring the gospel of grace to a remote island. Today, years later, the dolls' dresses are made on the island, the bodies of the dolls are made on another, and the dolls are sold or exported to the U.S. by HeartCraft in Denalia.

Threads of hope were still finding their way into the hearts of more and more people back in Denalia—including a young man named Budi. Like another person we'd rescued in the past, Budi was healing from a serious motorcycle accident. Because his leg had been improperly pinned back together, it became gangrenous. The doctor said he was in danger of losing it altogether. He lost his original job because of the accident, so he spent his time with us learning to sew. But his leg got worse and worse, and finally, the doctor decided to amputate. We were so sad to hear this. It was a horrible thought for Budi and for all of us.

Hearing the news, the believing staff in HeartCraft gathered around Budi's bed and prayed for his leg to be healed. They asked God for a miracle, knowing that's what it would take. Budi listened intently. The next day his leg showed such significant improvement that the doctor changed his mind. He decided he could keep working with it until it fully healed.

The news brought shouts of joy from those who prayed and from Budi himself. The Muslims all listened and watched intently. Everyone agreed that God had answered prayer. Budi eventually gave his heart to the Great Healer.

Nani was another person whom God touched through HeartCraft. A young mother, she had recently been through a horrible tragedy. Her little baby was sick with dysentery and became so dehydrated that Nani decided to take him to the hospital. Nusandians usually don't go to the hospital until they are losing all hope. To many, the hospital is considered a place where you go to die. Tragically, Nani's baby died in the public transport on the way to the hospital.

Overwhelmed with grief, Nani turned to Christians within the HeartCraft network for prayer and comfort. Nani accepted the Lord, and through her new relationships, she also learned a new skill. She made beautiful appliqué projects from her home.

210

Despite her loss, the Lord brought joy and encouragement into her life. In time she was blessed with other children.

Mrs. Winardi was a sweet older woman. Her husband was a retired army officer, but she was shy and rarely ventured out of her home. When we gave her the chance to work from her home, she jumped at the opportunity. With a little help, she designed a cute, fat clown to match the baby quilts that were being produced by HeartCraft. The clown had a little hat and a red nose. I wondered if it would sell. It did! Mrs. Winardi was so encouraged that she began to make a smaller version. I was skeptical if two different sizes would sell, but they did. Mrs. Winardi was another happy person to add to the list. One more life changed. Once again, love had found a way.

We helped another Kantoli lady, Mrs. Eti, get started making little stuffed beanbag bears. They were stuffed soft heads and their middle made of cute cloth and stuffed with corn kernels that we got from the market. Mrs. Eti's newly married son, Agus, liked to work with wood, though he had no training or particular experience. When Agus saw the beanbag bears that his mother was making, he gathered sticks from the forest and made little wooden benches for bears to sit on. They made an adorable set! Dewi and I took them to the shows, and they all sold.

One day we noticed a strange problem. The bears looked like they were getting skinny. When we looked closer and noticed the holes on the sides of the bears' bodies, we knew exactly what was happening! Rats! Rats had eaten right through the cloth in order to eat the corn filling! We had a good laugh and came up with a solution—we would put little pebbles in the body of the bears rather than corn kernels. They would be heavier, but safer. The rats would not be tempted to eat the rocks, and pebbles were cheaper anyway. We never had a problem again with the gravel-bag bears.

Anan was Steve's best friend from the university. He was a graduate with a BA degree in Kantoli language and history. When it came to the local language, he was the best. We had done research with Anan in Banteng a few years earlier when he was single, but now he was married, and he and his wife, Lia, had a little baby girl. We went to visit them, and we were shocked to see that this precious little girl was not gaining weight. She was very sickly and didn't have a healthy skin color. They took her to the doctor, and he ran some tests that showed their baby girl had a heart abnormality. She needed a heart operation to repair a valve in her heart. Without this surgery, she was not expected to live very long.

For a poor person, news like this is nothing short of overwhelming. Of course there is no health insurance in Nusandia, and the young family was already struggling to pay rent and put food on the table. Anan's government salary at the local tourism office was about $50 a month.

As we had done for so many others, we offered them a job through HeartCraft. Together we designed a little stuffed lamb. We transported big bags of leftover stuffing to their distant town, four hours away. We gave Lia cloth, and Deki trained her and Anan how to make the sheep. They turned out really well and began to sell. They made sheep until they were literally "counting sheep" in their sleep. Every little lamb they made would help toward the cost of the operation their little girl required. After a few months, she had a successful operation. It worked! She was healed. A little act of love had gone a long way.

When I thought I had no more ideas, Mrs. Ani came to my doorstep. She was a new widow with four children. How was I going to tell her that I didn't have any more ideas or any more cloth to create a new product? There was no way. I had to think of something else so that this woman could support her family. Ani came into the garage with me, and I showed her the smallest of scraps of cloth that were leftovers from the dolls and other things. They were really small—maybe too small. How would she make something from these? I gave them to her and she came back with what was to be one of my favorite products. She had made the smallest quilt I had ever seen—a tiny quilted key chain! They were really nice and inexpensive to make and to sell.

We were thrilled to see small groups of believers begin to emerge.

The Lord takes even the smallest of scraps from our lives and makes something beautiful out of them, for His glory. Ministries like HeartCraft make a spiritual impact in part because of the atmosphere they create. In our work environment, Muslims and Christians could work together and recognize each other as real people. They were equals, without pretense or discrimination. Normally in a context like this, Muslim neighbors oppress Christians, but in this case, the Christians had something to offer. They were offering jobs to Muslims—something quite rare. Giving jobs to the very people that persecute them? The effect is powerful. The Muslim can experience the love of Christ and be drawn to it, provided the believer lives a life that is Christ-like.

We were not asking Muslims to come inside a church build-ing. Rather we wanted to meet a very real need right in the community and to relate to them with respect, as friends and coworkers. In so doing, Christians could share their faith in a more natural, non-threatening way. They didn't have to be so afraid of losing their jobs.

I was energized by the deep relationships that emerged.

Another opportunity to mix believer with unbeliever was our training program. These meetings were the best way to get people from the village areas into the city so that we could all be together. There were training programs for those with beginner, interme-diate and the highest-level quilting skills. But the most important sessions were when we trained the staff leadership how to love—and reach the people with the gospel. This was important because some of the staff leadership were not Kantoli. They had come from other parts of Nusandia and needed to be trained how to specifi-cally love and reach the Kantoli people. The Kantoli, like all the other people groups in Nusandia, had their own unique culture and personality. It was important to relate to them on that basis.

In addition to special field trips during our training sessions, we took the staff to places they had never been before, such as the zoo. We even took them to the Kantoli retreats that were sponsored by the Lampstand staff. Here the workers—most of whom were not believers—saw large groups of Kantoli Christians performing their own cultural dances, songs, comedies and dramas—all in their own language. It was a time to eat and celebrate together. And of course they would hear special speakers—gifted evangelists who would explain the gospel in their own language. Perhaps most powerful of all, they would listen to the stories of Christians who had been persecuted for their faith but stood strong.

Chapter 17

LETTING GO

Those who plant in tears will harvest with shouts of joy.
They weep as they go to plant their seed,
but they sing as they return with the harvest.

—PSALM 126:5-6 NLT

Throughout 1995 and 1996, momentum continued to build with HeartCraft and our many other ministries. By this time, HeartCraft was five years old, and we employed approximately 400 men and women. The ministry was generating hundreds of thousands of dollars each year in quilt and craft sales—between $1 million and $2 million since I first opened the box from the Senders in North Carolina. A large building was designed as a center for all the activity, and a bus brought workers each day from their distant homes.

Remarkably, HeartCraft had grown with almost no outside capital or investment. Linda Ryan had given $3,000 to rent the first house that we used as a production center—the one that almost burned down. The second year, we borrowed $10,000 from the parents of one of our team members. We were able to pay this off completely within about six months. A few donors contributed $200 or $300 each, from time to time, to purchase additional sewing machines. Of course, this does not take into consideration the voluntary involvement of other members of our team and the value of my time and Steve's time, but it was still a remarkable story of growth with very minimal capital investment.

How did HeartCraft grow so fast in an environment where there were many spiritual and cultural hurdles to overcome? There is no question that we worked very hard. We also applied good business principles along the way. Although our overriding motivation was a spiritual one, we felt that God would honor good, ethical business practices. More important than any of these things, however, is the simple power of prayer—not only our own prayers, but the earnest prayers of many supportive friends back home in the United States and Canada. It was truly a work in which we were stretched to the limit, yet we felt God's favor.

Momentum was building, but at the same time, Steve and I were experiencing increased difficulty maintaining our residence visa. This is the document that foreigners living in Nusandia must have in order to live there long term, and it's something that foreign workers often struggle with when they live and work in developing countries. It is easier to stay in a country if one is working for an oil company or making a lot of money in a commercial enterprise. Even then, two or three years may be the limit, and Steve and I had been in the country ten years.

While we are always thankful when individuals are able to launch businesses in developing countries, we had chosen legally to develop HeartCraft as a local not-for-profit enterprise. HeartCraft had a local board of directors made up of Nusandian men and women. There were a number of reasons we chose this route. First, Nusandia has always ranked high on the list of corrupt countries. There are significant temptations for individual owners of an enterprise to abscond with all the money at some point. Second, we wanted local as well as Western donors to be able to contribute to the project at any time, with the assurance that their contributions were not enriching a single individual. Third, we really wanted all the participants in HeartCraft to benefit from the project's success.

We had maintained residency in various ways over the years—studying at a local university, teaching at a large English academy and consulting with a local manufacturer. Because these jobs normally lasted only two or three years, we were now wondering once again about the future.

That was the "push," but there was also an important and simultaneous "pull." This involved our mission organization, Pioneers, which had grown rapidly. There were now about 500 workers serving in 40 countries. Two organizations, each with offices in Australia and New Zealand, had expressed interest in joining our international ministry network. Steve had been asked to move to Australia for a period of time to help transition these new organizations into Pioneers.

Looking at all the factors, we concluded it might be good if we left the country for a period of time and then returned in a year or two. I was expecting my fourth child, so I was especially anxious to know where I would deliver the baby!

As we were weighing our options, Steve traveled to the U.S. for mission leadership meetings. I was left with the girls and a house full of workers, but I never felt lonely or worried, even though my due date was approaching. In fact, my mother came out to be with me once more. Two friends, Terri and Lynn, were available to help me if I went into labor while Steve was gone. Both were registered nurses and members of our team. Terri's training was in pre-natal and delivery. I was in good hands and did not anticipate any problems.

Steve finished his meetings in Orlando and started his long flight back to Nusandia. While transiting the San Francisco airport, he called me to make sure everything was okay. I told him I was having no contractions and was sure the baby would wait until he got back to Nusandia. After all, it was only a matter of 24 hours before he would arrive home.

No one told the baby, however. Later that very evening, as Steve was high over the Pacific, my contractions started to come. I tried to ignore them, but they kept getting stronger. At 4:00 a.m., I woke my mother, who quickly got up and started to pack. I called my dear friend Jada (one of the nine college students who visited us ten years earlier), who ran up the hill to watch the other girls. By the time she got to my home, I was almost ready to deliver!

Lynn came by to get Mom and me, and we rushed to the delivery clinic, weaving past early morning worshipers, traffic and pedestrians. The day starts early in the tropics! At one point I almost could not take it any longer. Lynn wanted to know if she should pull over on the side of the road to deliver the baby. I couldn't stand the thought of spectators watching and pointing while a white woman had a baby in the back seat of a car, so I urged her to drive a little faster. We made it just in the nick of time! Less than a half hour after we pulled into the clinic driveway, I was holding our fourth little girl, Victoria Grace, in my arms. And Steve was probably sound asleep somewhere over the Pacific!

I was proud of myself for delivering a baby so rapidly. The midwives were the same women who had helped in the delivery of the other three girls. In the past they had talked openly about how long it took me to deliver my babies because I was a weak American who didn't know how to work hard. Labor for my first baby, Joy, had been more than 30 hours! This time they smiled and commended me for having become a true Nusandian.

When Steve landed at the city airport later that afternoon, our older girls and Steve's cousin Tim, who also worked in Nusandia at the time, waved a huge sign from the airport veranda: "Victoria wants to meet her daddy." As Steve stepped off the plane onto the tarmac, he could hardly believe his eyes. Little Victoria had already been born, and he had missed it! That was so typical of our lives in those fast-paced years. We laughed together at how a baby just can't wait. Thank God, all went well.

Dewi holds a newborn Tori.

Soon after Tori was born, we got her a passport and headed for the airport. We needed to go to Singapore to renew our visas (For some reason they couldn't be renewed inside the country). When the immigration officer looked through Tori's brand-new passport, he noticed there was no entry stamp. He glanced at the baby and then at us and asked, "When did she enter the country?"

"Three weeks ago," Steve replied.

"Where's her entry stamp?" the officer asked, flipping through the pages once again.

"There is no stamp," Steve explained. "She was born three weeks ago.

The officer just shook his head. "Oh, that's a big problem."

"How big?"

"Really big. You can't have a baby on a visitor's pass."

"No one ever told us that," Steve replied, maintaining a polite voice. Having grown up in this country, nothing ever seemed to bother him. "The baby's already here. What should we do?"

"You can't get on the plane. You need to go immediately to the immigration office downtown."

With that we turned our young family of six around and headed home again on public transport. Then Steve drove his motorcycle to the immigration office. It was a dark, depressing, smoke-filled old building where large amounts of money exchanged hands in sealed envelopes. It was a place Steve had visited often over the years. He knew it well enough to bring plenty of reading material with him.

The wait was indeed a long one, punctuated by brief interviews in which one official or another would seek clarification on how the baby was born and then comment on how "big" this problem was. Steve would then enquire as to "how big" the problem might be. The officials were hesitant to put a dollar figure on it, not wanting to underestimate the amount this helpless foreigner might be willing to pay. It was a test of wills, to see who would wear out first, and how much money they could get out of Steve. Of course there were no written rules about such things. Steve finally settled on a $20 penalty for having a baby in the country illegally. The loss of our airplane tickets was actually a far greater penalty. We passed the airport immigration official again the next day, this time with a real baby in our arms.

After that visit to Singapore, we returned to Nusandia to put things in motion for our move. After more than ten years in Nusandia, this would be a big change. Steve would be able to fulfill his area director role for Pioneers from Melbourne, Australia, visiting Nusandia and other parts of Asia. We looked forward to the day when we could return to resume our work there.

The news of our soon departure hit our teammates and our HeartCraft staff and friends hard. While it was not completely unexpected, it ended up being rather sudden because of our visa dilemma. They had good, stable leadership with Faith and her team. Jane and others were available to help. The time had come for me to support them from a distance in any way that I could.

We set our departure date for a month later. We sold or gave away everything we had. We only planned to take a few suitcases with us to Australia and would not try to ship anything. It was hard for me to see the little white crib go out the door. We'd had it custom made, and all four of our girls had used it. In fact, Tori was still using it—she was only eight months old. Thankfully it would be a blessing to another young couple.

Goodbyes were painful. Our international team of more than 40 people hosted a wonderful banquet for us and gave us an album full of appreciation letters. Many of our Nusandian friends couldn't keep the tears back. That made me cry, too. It seemed like the end of an amazing era—a decade packed full of adventure, disappointment and answered prayer. Things would never be quite the same.

One of our dear women friends wept aloud and chased our car down the street for an entire block as we drove away. My tears, too, flowed freely.

Tati, Lili and Karen came with us to the airport, and it was especially sad to say goodbye to them. They would soon be carrying the vision to new places. I had enjoyed working with them so very much.

Shortly after our move to Australia, Nusandia, along with several other Southeast Asian nations, sank into a period of serious political and economic instability. Wild currency fluctuations took a toll, and as people's purchasing power plummeted, riots broke out in large cities. At the same time, Muslim activists took advantage of the instability to launch a wave of attacks on Christians throughout the country. On some eastern islands, Christians were hunted down and killed by the thousands and their churches burned to the ground. Hundreds of churches were destroyed over a period of two or three years. Such events rarely made it into the Western press. It would take 9/11, three years later, to finally awaken the outside world to the realities of Islamic radicalism that Nusandian Christians had been experiencing for years.

While we were in Australia, Faith stayed in touch with me by e-mail. In one of her messages, she mentioned an incident that saddened my heart. While Dewi was helping some customers at the store who were making an unusually large purchase, Dewi pocketed some of the money. It was not a large amount, but nevertheless she did pocket it and did not write everything on the receipt. Dewi was going through a time of serious financial need. Thinking it wouldn't be noticed, she had stolen a percentage of the sale—just a few dollar's worth—to help herself through a difficult time. When Faith confronted her, Dewi began to cry. Faith told Dewi that she wanted her to think about what this might mean. Dewi knew that her job could be terminated, even after all these years.

Faith thought and prayed for a few days before deciding how to respond to Dewi's moral lapse. Finally she decided to forgive Dewi and allow her to continue her work at the store. Dewi was surprised and thankful for the grace that was extended to her. She could see that Faith loved her and was being merciful.

In my many conversations with Dewi, one thing that she found especially hard was the idea that she needed a Savior. Dewi had long taken pride in being a person of exceptional moral character. She was convinced that she was a good person, especially in contrast to most of the people around her. She didn't feel particularly sinful; therefore, she didn't recognize her need of God's forgiveness.

I was distraught to hear the news, but Faith had another perspective. "I think God will use this in Dewi's life," Faith reassured me. "It was a painful experience, but it may be the very thing that she needs."

Sure enough, following this event, a deep sense of conviction settled over Dewi. She began to realize that she couldn't keep all of God's standards in her own strength. The longing for a savior, whatever the cost, grew in her heart.

After our 18-month assignment in Australia ended, we returned to the U.S. to visit my family in Orlando, Steve's family in Southern California, and our many friends and churches around the United States. In 1999 we were scheduled to return to Nusandia. Our bags were all packed when, rather suddenly, the Pioneers board asked if Steve would consider serving as president of Pioneers in the USA. We prayed earnestly about it and felt God's confirmation to accept the challenge. Our greatest heartache was the realization that we would not be returning to Nusandia and that our daughters would have to grow up in America rather than Nusandia.

In our new role, God broadened our horizons considerably, yet it was thrilling to keep up with what God was doing in Nusandia. Late one night, I received a phone call that would warm my heart forever. It was Dewi—and this was her first experience making an international telephone call. She spoke excitedly and rapidly because she could afford only three or four minutes on the line. Dewi told me that she had gone to one of the Kantoli retreats sponsored by Lampstand. There she had given her heart to Jesus Christ!

I could hardly believe my ears. After seven years of friendship and hundreds of conversations, God had finally answered the prayers of my heart.

Some of the quilters gather at a HeartCraft retreat.

Dewi had heard the testimony of a Kantoli Christian who was persecuted for her faith. That woman showed Dewi the scars on her back—scars she'd received while being beaten for trusting Christ. Dewi told me how the woman was radiant as she spoke. If that woman could walk a road of suffering as a Christian and still be joyful, Dewi wanted to follow Christ, too. That was the moment Dewi prayed to receive the Lord.

Now she was calling me to tell me the great news. "Thank you, Lina and Steve," she said. "Thank you for making the sacrifice to come and share the gospel with me. Thanks for not giving up!" She was crying and so was I.

"If you had never come, I would have never known the path to heaven. Now I am a changed person, forever."

Dewi displays one of her handmade wall hangings.

For several years following that call, we would get a call from Dewi once a year—on the anniversary of her spiritual salvation! Reflecting on it, I am glad that it was another Kantoli woman who had the privilege of being the last link in the chain of Dewi's spiritual journey. There is something special about a Kantoli leading another Kantoli to Christ. After all, that's what we've dreamed and asked God for—a chain reaction of faith among people we love.

After her decision to follow Christ, Dewi shared her faith wherever she went. She joined a small Kantoli fellowship of believers and started memorizing hundreds of passages of Scripture. "I can't make it without God's word in my heart," she explained to me on one of my recent visits back to Nusandia. Dewi was baptized in front of her Muslim family with many other Muslims looking on. Though small in stature, she is a woman of unusual faith and courage. It's just what I expected she'd be like when she finally decided to take the most important step of her life.

Chapter 18

TODAY AND BEYOND

- - - - - - - -

*My ambition has always been to preach the Good News where
the name of Christ has never been heard, rather than where a
church has already been started by someone else.*

—ROMANS 15:20 NLT

Surprising as it may sound, HeartCraft was just one part of
what God was doing. At the same time that HeartCraft was
expanding, Steve and I—and our co-workers—were involved in
projects that involved dozens and sometimes hundreds of people:
training programs, English schools, church-planting initiatives,
contextual ministries of various kinds, publications, radio and
TV broadcasts, community development initiatives and many
more. Yet, HeartCraft obviously holds a special place in my heart.

The HeartCraft story has been a big part of my personal
adventure with God. It was my opportunity to sink roots into
another culture and to develop deep relationships with a cir-

cle of new friends. Although they live in a very different context and have a very different worldview, these people are very dear to me. It was also a time when God became even more real and precious to me. HeartCraft was the laboratory in which I sought specific miracles from God and learned to trust Him as he performed a transformative and supernatural work in my life and the lives of others.

There was tremendous pain and hardship along the way. The victories didn't come without a cost. At times I felt it wasn't worth the personal price that I was paying, and there were many times when I felt completely inadequate for the job in front of me, but as I studied Scripture, I saw that the Lord deliberately used people who felt that way. Moses, for example, was that kind of person. He didn't feel he was the right man for the job. Even David was a shepherd boy, but God used him. Ruth was used by God even though she was a simple Moabite woman. Mary, Jesus' mother, was probably in her teens when she gave birth to Jesus. She didn't ask for the scandal or the sorrow that she experienced. The disciples were uneducated fishermen who went on to change the world. People like these remind me of my grandmother's scraps of cloth. They appeared worthless, but when woven together with threads of grace, they produced a beautiful quilt.

When God led Steve to his Orlando leadership role in Pioneers, I wondered once again what God had in store for me. The answer wasn't long in coming. Friends all around the world began contacting me. Many were people who had started projects similar to HeartCraft, or were thinking of doing so, and they needed help of one kind or another. They wanted advice on product choice, insights on working with the cultural challenges in developing countries and tips on how to market their products in the U.S. and other countries. They had heard that I was having success in selling HeartCraft quilts on the American market. In time, I once again sensed the Lord opening a door, this time to launch HeartCraft in the U.S.A., as a ministry that would advise and assist small- and medium-sized enterprises all around the world.

After nearly two decades, the HeartCraft experience has not ended. It goes on multiplying. Like the kingdom seed that Jesus talked about in the Gospel of Mark, this seed has taken on a life of its own.

The busy workroom at HeartCraft in Nusandia

One of the main purposes of HeartCraft is to connect the Christian public in the U.S. with isolated church-planting projects in places like China, Central Asia or northern India. Our team hosts craft sales while sharing the amazing stories of what God is doing in the various locations where these products are made. HeartCraft is a subsidiary of Pioneers, the ministry that my Dad and Mom started in our home thirty years ago—today a large and exciting global mission organization. All sales revenue from HeartCraft is channeled back into the projects and into expanding the network even further afield.

How long HeartCraft will survive in Nusandia, under growing economic pressure, only God knows. That's in His hands, not mine. Even if it does not endure in its present form, I have the joy of knowing that hundreds of lives have been impacted. The ripple effect will never be stopped. All the sacrifice and effort has been worthwhile.

Many friends in the West can relate to the personalities, struggles and victories that I experienced. They laugh when I tell them that, to this day, I've still never had the time to make a quilt myself! Yet, by God's grace, I've seen thousands of quilts and other crafts produced and sold by people who had no prior skill or business experience. People appreciate the business aspects of my story and the need to convey the gospel message in deed as well as in word. They recognize the logic of developing ministry models that are sustainable and provide material as well as spiritual direction. Some forms of missionary work are harder to relate to, but teaching life-sustaining skills such as sewing to disadvantaged people is something everyone can appreciate.

I do not claim to be a linguist, cultural anthropologist or business expert. I've simply been a devoted friend to the Kantoli. Some have asked if, looking back, I would have done anything differently. Not really. I have no major regrets. I let my life get more complicated than many may have thought wise, but I am glad that I did.

In November 2001, Steve and I visited China. Concluding our trip in Beijing, we boarded a flight bound for Tokyo, Minneapolis and eventually our home in Orlando. As we settled into our seats, an American woman struggled to get her three children into their seats across the aisle from us. Steve stood to help her lift her bags into the overhead compartment. He noticed out of the corner of his eye that the youngest child was wrapped in a very familiar looking quilt. Pointing to it, he asked the lady where she'd found such a beautiful quilt.

"It's a long story," she answered with a smile. "My husband is an oil company executive. Several years ago a young lady named Faith visited our isolated oil camp, bringing dozens of beautiful quilts with her. She told us amazing stories about a 'quilt lady' who taught her people how to sew. The quilts were so beautiful that I decorated my whole house with them! This is one of the quilts that I bought."

Steve smiled as the woman told her story. Nodding toward me he asked her, "Would you like to meet the Quilt Lady?"

Arlene with Dewi in 2006

The Richardsons dressed in traditional Kantoli clothing

ABOUT
THE AUTHOR

Arlene Richardson is founder of HeartCraft, an organization that helps people in need by marketing products from small- and medium-sized enterprises in the developing world. She is also involved in Pioneers, a mission organization with work in 95 countries.

Arlene and her husband, Steve (president of Pioneers-USA), have four daughters. When not speaking and sharing the vision of HeartCraft, Arlene enjoys using her gifts of hospitality and encouragement.

Arlene is sometimes available to speak at churches, conferences or women's events. If you'd like to find out more, get involved or arrange a HeartCraft presentation, you can contact Arlene by visiting: *HeartCraft.org* or *Pioneers.org* or by writing to her at:

HeartCraft@orlandoteam.com
Pioneers
10123 William Cary Drive
Orlando, FL 32832
407-382-6000

CPSIA information can be obtained at www.ICGtesting.com
Printed in the USA
LVOW06s0822121115

462195LV00002B/2/P